HOODOO FOR BEGINNERS

*Connect To The Ancient Spirit
World of Africa & Manifest
Success With Spells, Root
Magic, Conjuring, Herbs,
Traditions, History & More*

HISTORY BROUGHT ALIVE

FREE BONUS FROM HBA: EBOOK BUNDLE

Greetings!

First of all, thank you for reading our books. As fellow passionate readers of History and Mythology, we aim to create the very best books for our readers.

Now, we invite you to join our VIP list. As a welcome gift, we offer the History & Mythology Ebook Bundle below for free. Plus you can be the first to receive new books and exclusives! Remember it's 100% free to join.

Simply scan the QR code to join.

FREE DOWNLOAD

CONTENTS

INTRODUCTION

❧

What is Hoodoo? Black magic, spells and conjuring, the art of healing through herbs? Ancestral rituals, talking to the spirits—folk magic?

You have to decide once you have understood how this ancient craft works.

"Hoodoo for Beginners" takes you on a journey into the mystical world of Hoodoo, rootwork, or conjuring. It is a spiritual connection that was formed between higher powers, the elements, and oppressed African-American slaves who brought over beliefs and traditions from their native Africa.

It was a secret craft created among the long-suffering people to help them form a bond of protection with the help of higher beings and their dead ancestors. Hoodoo worked through practices that taught believers about invoking the blessings and help of spirits and deities; through persuasion powers, and knowledge of healing with herbs, rituals, spell casting, talismans, and roots.

The practice earned the taboo label. Because Hoodoo invoked fear among those who did not understand the true meaning and power of the craft. It was also a threat to the slave owners and slave minders who found the power of Hoodoo growing on the great southern plantations.

This book is for the beginner feeling a strong pull toward the traditional craft; curious to discover its heart, its lifeblood, and its rewards.

I am writing this book from personal experiences, having done more than dabble in the art of Hoodoo. Therefore, I offer you credibility. "History Brought Alive" is dedicated to creating a factual connection between the present and the past by exploring long feared folk magic, religions, and traditions.

Every book published by the company on history, mythology, and ancient crafts is backed by authenticated information to ensure the reader's eagerness to learn more about the mysticism surrounding our world is compounded with factual information. There are no hearsays or old wives' tales in this book.

Everything you learn here is related to the craft and backed by credible sources. I will not feed anyone's desire to make Hoodoo dark and feared—it is so much more than that.

At the end of this book, you will become an authority on the craft as you delve deeper into the exciting world of Hoodoo step by step.

The magic of hoodoo is not fictional, nor is it a religion. It is a part of the African-American heritage; a traditional folk craft born here in North America to flourish and nurture all who respect the immense power of forming a pact between the spiritual beings of the Earth.

Hoodoo conjure was a secret craft, a form of salvation and deliverance for the entrapped slaves in the South, but 400 years since the first slaves were brought over to America, how far and deep has Hoodoo reached?

I guess it's safe to say that the practice of hoodoo is so widely popular today that it could be looking you right over the shoulder, as the craft is gaining prominence once more among the younger generation. It is no longer a secret craft, but it is still shrouded in mystique and kept veiled so others are blissfully ignorant of the great power that followers of this ancient craft wield.

"Hoodoo for Beginners" starts at the beginning. Differentiate Hoodoo from Vodou, or Voodoo, a religion originating in Western Africa and Haiti having deep roots in African culture.

Let's explore the myths and facts surrounding the craft. I will help you to understand the true nature of rootwork so you can differentiate between unrealistic theories and stories cooked up to create fear and doubt by those who do not fully understand the positive influence of Hoodoos throughout the African-American culture.

I will present you with historical facts and authenticated stories that prove the might of Hoodoo. Through each chapter, you will learn about the essential conjurer's tools for creating a bridge between the elements and spirits to harness their power and find a doorway into the spiritual world.

Gris bags, talismans, magic candles, roots, hoodoo powder, etc. and rootworkers' tools are all explained in detail.

The traditions of Hoodoo dictate that before you can call on the power of Hoodoo tools, and the spirits you must first fathom their meaning; why, how, and when each tool used in Hoodoo conjuring came to be and its significance, and the spirits responsible for granting of favors. It is only through understanding that a spiritual connection is formed between a man, the spirit world, and objects of power.

In the beginning, the heritage and roots of every African-American, lie the secrets and power of present-day Hoodoo. Are you ready to begin your journey of discovery and empowerment?

CHAPTER 1
THE HISTORY OF HOODOO UNRAVELED

The transatlantic slave trade which created the African diaspora is greatly responsible for the birth of Hoodoo in North America. The African diaspora refers to the mass displacement of the native African people.

Hoodoo is often associated with the practice of "conjure" giving way to the popular term Hoodoo Conjure. However, Hoodoo is more than mere magic and spells.

The Antebellum era saw an influx of slaves arriving on southern plantations in North America. A majority of them worked in the fields. They were underfed, ill-treated, and lived in cramped quarters. They were no more than tools brought to serve the needs of the rich white plantation owners.

Towards the middle half of the 1800s Protestant Evangelicalism, was offered, not by choice, as a form of salvation to save the soul and many black slaves were converted to Christianity. However, unknown to the slave minders and slave owners the African people brought to work in slavery in southern plantations brought with them the knowledge of ancient religions. The worship of saints, spirits, and dead ancestors.

The religion of Vodou originated in Western Africa and is a base on which Hoodoo was formed, although not in its entirety. The Christianity-converted slaves discovered similarities between traditional African religions and Christian beliefs. They were desperate for a source of salvation, other than what was preached at the African-American church. They needed a weapon to fight back and also a practice to seek refuge in and have their desires granted. Hoodoo was born from these needs. But Vodou/Voodoo prevalent in Haiti was banned, and so was the practice of Hoodoo. This further compounded the practice of the craft in shadowy quarters, far away from the prying eyes of the slave minders.

Therein begins the misconception that Hoodoo is to be feared, associating the practice with evil intent. The belief is that Hoodoo is all about the desecration of graves, zombies, and the creation of spells and hexes to cause harm. The stigma attached to Hoodoo has prevented those practicing the craft from openly declaring the true intent of this traditional North American practice which is a marvelous synthesis of religions, native knowledge, and traditional beliefs prevalent among the diverse ethnicities on the North American continent.

Hoodoo is not to be confused with Voodoo—or Vodou—although all practices have emerged from African culture. Instead, Hoodoo has its roots in Christianity. With more similarities to Christianity that is let on.

Hoodoo was branded as superstition. The label is awarded to any practice for which the masses do not have a proper understanding. In other words, a practice that is not a mainstream belief.

Let's not forget that in ancient Rome, Christianity was banned similarly. Treated like a cult following, and those who practiced Christianity did so in secret, holding mass in hidden quarters fearing the punishment that followed anyone who was found out to be a believer of Christ.

The practice of Hoodoo Conjure did not soar to the heights of popularity that Christianity did;

the practice remains in the shadows, although modern followers no longer hide their beliefs.

To understand the roots of Hoodoo in America, we must first look at its beginnings which were amongst the African slaves who followed the teachings, rituals, and customs of the West African religion of Voodoo.

In this chapter, we will look at the evolution of hoodoos on the North American Continent. How a practice shrouded in superstition bearing a reputation of being evil, survived over the centuries to become a folk religion in the US. Is it possible this traditional craft has gained its strength through time by integrating its beliefs through culture?

It's safe to establish that Hoodoo survived mainly due to its acceptance as a sort of folk religion. Which relies on beliefs, rituals, and practices being passed on from one generation to the next as a traditional cultural heritage.

Still, Hoodoo is not a religion, it is a heritage; therefore, when you seek to know more about Hoodoo you are delving deeper into the legacy, traditions, practices, and culture of the African—American slaves and their descendants.

How it All Started, Vodou and Hoodoo? The Beginnings

The African diaspora is mainly responsible for the birth of Hoodoo conjure or rootwork in North America. In case you have not heard of the term, let me explain.

The African diaspora refers to the mass displacement of the native African people.

Millions fell prey to the slave trade which flourished between 1500 to 1800. People from Central and Western Africa were forcefully taken to feed the Transatlantic Slave Trade, ending up across the American continent; with the Caribbean acting as a hub from where many were transhipped to the Americas.

The first slaves to enter North America came to Virginia in 1619. And so the South became the most prominent North American region for slavery, and subsequently, the birthplace of Hoodoo.

Hoodoo became both a protector and weapon for fighting against the injustices suffered by the African-American people. Freed slaves and those still in bondage relied on Hoodoo as a form of spiritual healing. It was a link to their African heritage and also a weapon to rebel against their oppressors.

The practice of "conjure" came with the African slaves, but before we move on to Hoodoo Conjour it is important to understand the traditions, beliefs, and customs of connecting religions that served as a base for the formation of Hoodoo.

How Much Do You Know About Vodou?

I would describe Vodou as the seed from which Hoodoo came into existence.

Vodou is an ancient belief; a religion that originated in the Western African nations of South Benin, Nigeria, and Togo—the region was called the Kingdom of Dahomey up until the 1970s, now called Benin.

Another name for Dahomey is *Fon*, it is also the name of the language used by the Dahomey people who are known as *Fon nu*.

Fon is similar to *Ewe*, a language spoken in South Togo, South Benin, and Ghana, it is known as the common language among the *Kwa* people who come from the Niger-Congo region.

Vodou is the Fon name for 'spirit' or 'god' and is also spelled as Vodou or Vodon. It is a singular religion practicing the worship of one almighty deity. Hence, Vodou is based on monotheism. Much like Christianity.

Mawu-Lisa the pantheon of all deities also called Mahou-Lisa, or Mahu-Lisa refers to the female deity *Mahu/Mawu* and *Lisa* her husband— the creators.

In Dahomey mythology, the pair are one— described as the sun and the moon. Vodou is the worship of one primary deity (monotheism). Or in this case the creators of heaven and earth.

The female entity *Mawu* is the moon. She symbolizes night; together with fertility, motherhood, joy, gentleness, forgiveness, and rest. These are, as you will notice, the epitome of the female gender.

Lisa is the sun; the male entity. He is associated with the day; war, strength, toughness, power, and steadfastness. A paragon for the stronger sex.

In Haitian Vodou, this supreme entity is known as *Gran Met* or *Bondye/Bonye.* An all-powerful God who is also transcendent.

The New-World Afro-diasporic vein of Vodou practiced in Haiti is a combination of European, African, and traditional Taino religious beliefs. The Taino are an indigenous race of people from the Caribbean. Most sources link Vodou's beginnings to Haiti. Where the craft evolved and became stronger among the slaves working in the direst of conditions on the vast plantations there.

Vodou in Haiti

Haitian Vodou emerged around the 16th century; it began as an amalgamation of traditional West African beliefs and Christianity which was fast spreading through colonization. Therefore, *Bondye* quite often shares a link with the God of Christianity, who is identified as the beginning and the end. The all-powerful in whose hands lie the fate of men.

However, Vodou is not as straightforward as explained thus far.

Contradicting the theory of Vodou being a monotheistic religion there is a belief in spirits. Deity worship in African culture is categorized as the worship of primary, secondary, and tertiary gods. Therefore, the *Lwa*, pronounced as *Iwah*, exists as part of Vodou's polytheistic belief in secondary gods.

The lwa are called by many names, loa, loi, mystères, saints, anges (angels), Les Invisibles. In Vodou, there are thousands of lwa who act as intermediates to Mawa-Lisa or Bondye on behalf of men. Again there is a similarity to Christianity where the intercession of saints and angels on behalf of man is a part of the belief.

Spirit Possession

An important element in Vodou is possession. Possession allows the lwa, to bond with a man.

Vodouism believes in the possession of a man's spirit/soul; possession is a method of unification between man and God.

Devotees go on to describe their experience of being possessed as "being ridden like horses by the lwa" they allow the lwa to take control of the reins. It is described as giving in to the desire of being owned by the spirits during the period of possession. This is seen as a means of fulfilling the desires of both the spirit and man. The possession by a spirit is often seen as a process of healing, divine intervention, and answers to one's problems.

The practice of Vodou is overseen by priestesses, known as the *mambo* or *manbo* (the latter is a derivation of the Fon word for 'mother of magic'—*nanbo).* The male equivalent is an *oungan.*

In both the Western African and Haitian versions of Hodou, it is the priestess who oversees the rituals, prays for healing, and intercedes as a bridge between the gods, and the spirits, on behalf of the faithful. Initiation into the priesthood requires a series of trials to be performed. Increasing the priest's *konesan,* (their sacred knowledge) is the ultimate goal of each trial.

Vodou is a structured religion; a complex web of intricately woven traditions, rituals, and beliefs. It is important to understand these basics for you to get a grasp of where Hoodoo begins.

One final point I wish to make before moving on is the clarification of the term Voodoo. The more popular and glamorized name was given to the folk religion predominantly by Hollywood.

Voodoo a Carefully Constructed Image of Black Magic, Vengeance, and Death

The name Voodoo invokes images of black magic rituals, dolls stuck with pins, graveyards, and zombies for many. Fear and dread are associated with the name which is a carefully marketed brand to keep the image of evil associated with the craft.

In English, Creole, and French, the correct term for the religion is Vodou, derived from the fon name of *Vodoun.* The derogatory term in which the name Voodoo is used emerged around the

1920s after the 1915 occupation of Haiti by the US.

Voodoo grew in popularity as people lapped up the bacchanalias-type rituals, witchcraft, and evil sorcery associated with Voodoo presented as an uncivilized religious practice on the island. The image was given prominence through the movies and carefully spun stories; the American public lapped it all up with eager disgust.

Therefore, the name Voodoo to this day is associated with evil black magic with the intent of harm; the association of the ancient religion with Christianity is lost in the perverted image of Vodou through Voodoo.

Many believe the US occupation of Haiti at the time was responsible for this twisted portrayal of Vodou as a means to justify the actions of the US government.

Here's what Professor of Arficology Patrick Bellegarde-Smith, from the University of Wisconsin-Milwaukee had to say.

"The word 'voodoo' comes out of Hollywood in the 1920s, '30s, '40s as the United States was occupying Haiti, and it served to justify the occupation to a large extent in the eyes of Americans," (VodouOrVoodoo, n.d.)

CHAPTER 2
THE BIRTH OF HOODOO

Hoodoo, Conjure, or Rootworking all refer to the same ancestral practice or craft born in North America. Hoodoo evolved from a need, a need for the protection and salvation of the African slave suffering under dire conditions in a foreign land.

The people of Africa, stolen from their homeland brought with them the knowledge of an ancient folk religion—Vodou. Which was highly prevalent in Haiti, a hub for the dispersion of slaves to the North American continent.

Healing, divine intervention, and spiritual protection is the promise of Hoodoo, and not the corrupted version viewed in the US of black magic, hedonism, casting hexes, and sorcery used for evil purposes against society.

Vodou, an ancient religion, was already being viewed as a primitive form of evil magic practiced in Africa. It was convenient for slave owners to categorize the practices of the enslaved people as evil and primitive as a means to justify the western imperialistic tactics adopted by slave traders; this perception was further endorsed by Christian missionaries intent on "saving the souls" of the primitive people practicing black magic.

The areas of North Carolina and Georgia were soon populated by African slaves brought in from the Congo and Angola regions. With them, they brought knowledge of ancient Western African folk religions. These people suffered many atrocities. They were tortured, starved, and overworked.

Therefore a great need, a huge hunger, for justice prevailed among the enslaved people of Africa, and it is from this enormous need that Hoodoo was born. Born out of the souls of dead slaves whose spirits empowered the first conjurers to discover the power and a weapon to fight back spiritually through Hoodoo.

Spirit worship dominated the African traditional religions; spirits of the dead ancestors, spirits of the land, and deities worshiped on the African continent were venerated. However, all that was going to change as the African slaves were influenced by the teachings and supernatural beliefs of the new religions and ethnicities they became exposed to.

The Influence of Christianity on Hoodoo

The Black Code or Code Noir governing slavery within the French colonies, declared, that slaves be baptized into the Christian religion.

The enslaved people were offered salvation in the form of forced baptism into Christianity. In doing so the missionaries unwittingly revealed to the African people that Christianity was quite similar to the deeply spiritual aspects awarded to Vodou, and other traditional religions born on the African continent.

The worship of one divine God, Mawu-Lisa, and the intervention of the lwa spirits, as is the belief of the *Fon nu* people of Dahomey had strong similarities to the supernatural characteristics of Christianity which too was centered on spirits and saints, Jesus Christ and a supreme God. Let me remind you once more about the similarity of Christianity centered on the Holy Trinity the Father, Son, and Holy Spirit. And of Voudon on the creators, the Sun and Moon (Mawu-Lisa).

The connection between the one true God of Christians, and Bondye/Grand Met, the supreme creator worshiped in Haitian Vodou, and the belief in spirits and saints led to the manifestation of a divine practice the enslaved people found comfort and safety.

It was a unique underground practice born among the African-American community using the fragments of their traditional ancestral religions from Africa, and the connection found in the teachings of European religions such as Christianity, as well as the native religious practices, and knowledge of herbalism from the indigenous people in the new land they were enslaved in, the Native American Indians.

As a practice shrouded in the European religion of Christianity, the enslaved people were thus able to follow their banned craft of hope and protection inside Black-American Christian churches and at the same time satisfy their capturers' needs to offer them salvation through Christianity. To this day, there are many Christian prayers used in the performance of Hoodoo rituals.

A fine example is how possession, a key component of Vodou and Hoodoo, was hidden in the open as part of the black American church culture.

The 'Christian' slaves practiced what was called "Catching the Holy Ghost." The term in Christianity's belief revolves around faith in saints and giving up one's spirit to the Holy Ghost to fulfill a desire or need which is very much how possession in Hoodoo works. And so, in this guise, the slaves were practicing possession in Hoodoo where spirits were invoked to take possession.

There are many similarities between Hoodoo and Christianity which the black slaves used to their advantage, mostly to avoid punishment and death which was the fate dealt out to anyone caught practicing the taboo religion of Voodoo.

Hoodoo saints and spirits were openly worshiped under the guise of Catholic saints; the supernatural entities were venerated while prayers and psalms similar to Christianity were used for healings and rituals.

African slaves who adopted the European religion of Christianity did not find it a necessity to abandon their traditional religious beliefs. Instead, they found a way to easily merge the two to form a new practice—Hoodoo.

Native American Influences in Hoodoo

Native Americans were among the first slaves in Louisiana, which was the homeland of the indigenous people of North America and the place where Hoodoo evolved.

The many Native American tribes that were held in bondage were soon joined by the African slaves brought over during the Transatlantic Slave Trade. As is to be expected, the two groups bonded, planning escape routes and sharing their traditional beliefs and knowledge of roots, herbs, and spirits that resided in the land, the animals, the rain, water, trees, and plants.

And so Hoodoo was born as a marvelous amalgamation of African Traditional Religions, Native American beliefs and practices, folk magic, spirits of nature, the divine intervention of saints, supernatural powers, and Christianity. The dominant characteristics of Hoodoo, however, come from African Traditional Religions. Although Hoodoo is more a native North American practice while Vodou is traditional African folk religion.

The New American Folk Religions— Hoodoo

The practice was a combination of spirits from Haitian Vodou, the lwas and mystères, the archangels and saints from Catholicism, the spirits of the Native Americans, spirits of the ancestors, and of course zombies which you will learn more of when we explore the pantheon of Hoodoo.

It was a hearty mix of new spirits and those from traditional African beliefs. The supernatural was coupled with symbols, sacred rituals, dances, prayer, and songs also borrowed as an influence from other religious practices.

Therefore, it is largely believed that European customs and beliefs too had a great influence on the creation of Hoodoo.

Many evolutions took place among the African slaves exposed to the diverse religious and supernatural customs of the new land.

- Traditional African religious practices and rites seen as pagan rituals were largely abandoned.

- African words used in Hoodoo, compared to Vodou, became less and were replaced by English words. For example, in Vodou, a male priest is *houngan,* and a priestess *mambo* from the *Fon* language. But in Hoodoo you get the rootworker, the goopher doctor, the cunning man, the high man, and other typical English terms. They were best known as *Gullah* among the African slaves.

- African, Native American, and Christian supernatural customs were adopted to create magico-religious practices.

- The emergence of new beliefs, rituals, and customs takes into account elements from European religious beliefs, African traditional religions, and Native American myths and practices.

Hoodoo was a hybrid practice, a cross between cultures, a synthesis of beliefs with one purpose—improving and protecting the lives of enslaved black people, giving them hope and a better chance at achieving their desires.

Therefore, Hoodoo is a practice embedded with rituals for healing the body, mind, and soul, seeking divine intervention for good luck and well-being, and for the protection of the African-American community.

It is magico-religious; referring to a craft using magical practices to seek supernatural intervention for the granting of favors and obtaining specific needs.

Therefore, Hoodoo became the additional support when religion alone did not deliver and ease the suffering of the enslaved African-American community.

The Problem Rituals and Beliefs of the Black Slaves—Hoodoo

Authorities on Hoodoo emerged, and the practice spread widely, by the 19th century, among the enslaved African-American population.

Followers of the craft or Hoodooists were called many names; conjure women and men, root doctors, Hoodoo doctors, soothsayers, spirit workers, two heads, and so on and so forth. These authorities on Hoodoo were credited with having special knowledge of the spirit world, the sacred arts, roots, herbs, rituals, and granting blessings.

In Virginia and Maryland the term cunning doctors, high women/men was common as the more popular English or white man terms used for those who practiced "good magic".

There never were priests or priestesses, as there are in Vodou, but then Hoodoo is not a religion. It is a practice open to anyone as curious and devoted as you are to learn more about the divine powers that govern the power of Hoodoo.

Hoodoo grew in popularity as a secret practice among the enslaved black plantation workers at the height of slavery, and Hoodoo doctors, conjurers, or spirit workers with supernatural powers became popular; they were seen as a form of salvation and powerful rebellion against the slave masters.

These teachers or practitioners of Hoodoo were sought out by African-American society for many needs. For healing various types of physical ailments, offering protective spells against threatening forces such as the slave breakers, making people fall in love, improving one's fortune or riches, and even retrieving objects that were lost. They were the local folk doctors of sorts who performed "good magic" aiding the everyday needs of the black community.

However, there is good and bad to all magic, and Hoodoo Conjure is no exception. The exploited and vulnerable state of the oppressed black slaves led to the manifestation of a darker version of Hoodoo being practiced.

Let's not forget though that Hoodoo's purpose was the protection of the black slaves from harm, violence, and suffering. The belief that a higher power could be called on was needed for the healing of mind and body. Therefore, Hoodoo magic was used at times for revenge, retaliation, and also as a form of retaliation on behalf of the helpless.

Aggressive and threatening forms of magic, as well as cursing, are seen as heathen practices which belong to uncultured peoples and are therefore feared, and categorized as a taboo form of black magic. But, let me remind you that aggression and cursing are both present in other religions.

Christianity for example; one instance is where Noah saved the Israelis from bondage in Egypt after several aggressive acts against the Pharaoh and his people. The land was cursed several times with the death of the firstborns in all Egyptian homes being the final trial. Again, here is a fine example of spirituality, or faith, being used as a tool for the "greater good".

Hoodoo was always an underground practice, which at times hid in plain sight under Christian rituals. The stigma that was awarded to Vodou better known as Voodoo in its carefully constructed image of evil black magic was banned in North America.

Practicing conjure and Voodoo were seen as

venues for instigating rebellion amongst the slaves. The negative impact of the craft on the slave trade was taken quite seriously with legal action often being implemented to squash any possibility of an uprising.

A good example is when around the 19th century the governors of Louisiana banned the import of slaves from Santo Domingo and Martinique on the premise that they possessed a penchant for the practice of Vodou or Voodoo.

Segregating the Practise of Hoodoo

Let's break down the practice of Hoodoo.

Hoodoo has its roots in African Traditional Religions which focus on ancestral devotion, seeking spiritual protection, and herbal healing. The root work and herbal healing knowledge, as well as the power of spirits from nature, were learned from the Native Indians. While the supernatural aspect of Christianity greatly influenced and helped shroud the practice of the slave minders.

Root and Rootworking

This does not refer to working with roots alone as one would envision from the name.

Roots in the literal context will refer to the entire

plant and not just the root. It will include all parts of the plant including the seed, stem, and petals—think of 'root' as an umbrella term.

Rootwork in its entirety is the use of natural objects from nature similar to herbalism, as well as organic substances (including animals) for performing rituals, and spells to make events happen in relation to healings or even causing harm.

Hands—or gris bags—and Goopher dust, which is very much a part of traditional African magic, were for example made by root doctors to be used as talismans of protection and even for vengeance. The dust was collected from graveyards and the practice is considered one of the most important links Hoodoo retains with its African heritage.

Native American contributions toward the healing power a Hoodooist or root doctor possessed were wide. There was at least one Gullah (rootworker) on every plantation, and slaves put their trust in this healer while eyeing the white physicians with distrust.

The use of roots for both healing and casting spells was used, hence the name two heads were often given to rootworkers. The Ginseng root, a symbol of male fertility, was favored amongst the root doctors for both its curative powers, and as a vessel for supernatural influences. The "walking man" is often the reference given to a charmed ginseng root.

Divination or supernatural predictions too were achieved through rootwork. For example; if a root doctor was asked to put a root on a person, it would involve a supernatural element. In this ritual, goofer dust was turned into a powerful concoction of dried lizard or snake powder mixed with dirt from a graveyard. This was to be rubbed on the person seeking the favor, to cause harm to another, to prevent it from befalling the believer, or even make someone fall in love.

A rootworker had many skills; mojo bags were another method of offering supernatural protection/help for a specific purpose. Often a dime would be tied around the ankle or a small sack containing both plant and animal parts would be worn around the neck.

Hoodoo Conjuring

Conjur or conjuring—the casting of spells, refers to the bridge created between the spirits of dead people, angels, and saints as well as other divine beings from the spirit world.

Ancestors and even Jesus Christ as well as supernatural elements from Christianity will be included in Hoodoo Conjur. Factors that create that strong bond between Hoodoo and other traditional religions.

Although connected deeply to religion, "magic" has also garnered a lot of negative publicity throughout the ages. The persecution of witches throughout European history is testament enough to the huge element of fear created by black magic. Going back to the example of Moses; he was able to match the magic of the sorcerers in Pharaoh's court by turning water to blood, and his staff into a snake.

Practitioners and opponents of Hoodoo magic have over the ages acquired, recreated, and even criticized the craft. Although viewed as a vile opponent to orthodox religious beliefs, it is in fact a reflection of the essence on which most religions are based.

Powerful slaves who were known as conjure men/women gained the respect of their fellow slaves. But they were also sought out by the white slave owners who often visited them for their very accurate soothsaying powers. These conjure men wielded a sense of dark power and were often left alone by slave owners and slave minders who feared and believed the many stories of supernatural retaliation that were spreading in the south.

Modern Young African-American Christians Find a Connection With Hoodoo

Hoodoo which began to spread rapidly in the 1800s is an accepted and widespread practice in our modern times. Although the stigma of the practice being bad still sticks among the ignorant.

Scholars have researched the history of Hoodoo making a wealth of information available to the curious, which is no longer limited to just the African-American community.

Christian youth are trying to understand and connect with their African heritage. Most of that heritage happens to be linked to Hoodoo which to their surprise has deep links to Christianity making it easier for them to continue their Christian beliefs while delving deeper into their ancestral religions.

These youngsters are deciding for themselves, trying to dispel the myths put in place during the 18–19th centuries, by white supremacy, and the Christian churches, that Hoodoo and most traditional African religions are pagan rituals, dark and evil practices with an intent to harm.

They are exploring practices centered on traditional African cosmology, and at the same time learning about herbal healing powers, the power found within ancestral objects and communicating with spirits. Therefore, these youngsters are able to determine for themselves how the power of Hoodoo is used and its true context when it comes to determining its good and bad traits.

The Evolution of Hoodooism Over Time

The Antebellum era or you may better know it as the 'Great Plantation Period' is when Hoodoo really grew in strength. This was the time from around the mid-1800s to the beginning of the American Civil War which commenced in 1861.

The conjure men that evolved during this period offered the slaves protection from the cruel actions of the slave minders. These rootworkers offered protection together with other healing services, as well as supernatural services such as soothsaying.

As such their fame grew and so did their power with the strongest conjure men being left alone to go about their business as even the white slave minders feared their reputation.

Some of the famous conjure women and men

you should read up on include Dr. Buzzard, Aunt "Zippy" Tule, Aunt Caroline Dye, and Dr. Jim Jordan; they are not from the Antebellum era, instead, these powerful conjurers used their power and fame to both help the public and grow rich. For example, Jim Jordan was able to amass considerable wealth and owned numerous companies by the time he died in 1962.

The most loved was probably Aunt Caroline Dye who went on to become one of the most prominent conjure women in and around Newport, Arkansas; her soothsaying powers were renowned. Aunt Caroline Dye passed away in 1918 and is said to have used her powers for only good.

The Three Elements of Hoodoo

You may have asked yourself the question, "is Hoodoo real?" several times before deciding to pick up this book.

To everyone who has experienced the craft, yes it is.

However, you must come to that discovery on your own once you have journeyed through your learning process. I will go on to explain the three elements on which the craft of Hoodoo works, and gains the faith of its followers.

A religion becomes real through faith. You pray to Gods and saints because you believe they exist and are listening to you.

How your prayers are answered depends on the extent of your belief, and how deep and steadfast your faith is coupled with how much of the supernatural element you believe in without doubt or question.

Hoodoo, although not a religion, works along the same lines—it is real and based on trust and the virtue of those practicing the craft. It continues to exist and interact with believers, therefore it is real.

A craft that was formed as an amalgamation of several religions but not categorized as a religion is hard to fully comprehend. Yet Hoodoo has withstood the test of time not letting down believers.

To Understand How Hoodoo Made it Into the 21st Century Let's Look at Its Basic Elements

The enslaved people of Africa, many by then born into slavery in America and not Africa, toward the latter parts of the 1800s, started to rely on Hoodoo doctors for healing, physically and mentally.

The natural herbs and roots used by rootworkers as curative concoctions do in fact have strong connections to herbal medicinal remedies and offer the same curative promises the medicine prescribed by a physician does. Let's not forget that Hoodoo is also magico-religious, stepping in when religion fails to deliver.

The use of supernatural powers and conjuring offers the desired result where root doctors create talismans from roots and other objects to grant the seekers what they desire. In the past, these talismans, hands, and gris bags were quite often worn for protection against the slave breakers.

It was a case of fixing the mind to believe in the magic in order for it to work, although there are accounts registered by skeptics who witnessed the true power of an enchanted talisman.

Hoodoo Works and Manifests Its Powers on the Following Three Elements.

1. *The Use of Natural Organic Remedies for Healing*

Herbalism and other organic substances, as I mentioned before, are similar to those used by the Native Americans who shared their vast knowledge of the curative powers of herbs, roots, and plants.

2. *The Placebo Effect Functions on Faith and Perception.*

The belief in something that would otherwise be incomprehensible. Spells, concoctions, and magical talismans promise to give the seeker what they desire, mostly catering to a desire that would otherwise be hard to manifest on their own.

Belief makes the crafts' power real. Placebos can be inert procedures or objects which are used in Hoodoo rituals.

The mind plays a huge role in the success of Hoodoo magic. Therefore, the placebo effect works in the context of mind over matter—the power of suggestion.

People seeking the help of rootworkers value their power, place faith in their ability to deliver their desires, and are eager to follow instructions that lead to favorable results.

The belief in the conjure man/woman's power to heal is similar to the belief you place in contemporary doctors and the medicine they prescribe.

You believe the pills you ingest are going to make you well. In most instances, this psychological influence does make you feel better. Let's not forget the actual curative effect of the components in the medicine that work to heal. But believing in medicine makes you accept its curative abilities which do contribute to the healing process. This phenomenon is further compounded through studies proving its effects.

Hoodoo works in the same way, the believer's faith in the root doctor causes them to accept the spiritual healing promised, by opening their minds and placing trust in the supernatural which in part contributes to the remedy working.

3. *The Nocebo Effect, the Negative Phenomenon*

Now here's the flip side of the placebo effect, the negative aspect of believing in a favorable outcome. Here again, mind over matter works negatively to cause harm.

A nocebo effect is the harboring of negative thoughts that can cause harm to a person physically and mentally. Those thoughts could be self-achieved or planted in your mind through the power of suggestion.

Think about it, if a relatively healthy person is suddenly diagnosed with cancer, they are suddenly going to be burdened with the negative effects of the illness. Although they lived normal healthy lives before the diagnosis the implication of suffering from the terminal illness will cause rapid degeneration of their physical being. Because the mind has suddenly been told the body is unwell.

To prove the effects of the nocebo phenomenon, a study was conducted where some patients undergoing a test were told it would be painful while the rest were told it was a simple painless exercise.

The results proved the power of suggestion worked with the groups. The batch, already informed of the probability of pain, found the test 'painful' while the other half had no experience of discomfort (Pfingsten et al., 2001).

The power of suggestion when wielded by a clever Hoodooist can be quite influencing and damaging when used to cause mischief or to gain vengeance.

For example, a person being told that they are under a curse that will cause their death, will upon accepting the suggestion, let the thought corrupt their mental being which in turn will influence their physical being until death does become a reality. That is the power of suggestion and the third element on which Hoodoo works.

Despite Hoodoo having the power to cause harm, it is still a practice created to protect and nurture the well-being of the African-American community, although today Hoodoo offers protection to a wider spectrum of believers regardless of race.

It is still predominantly a healing practice much like that of a physician. The rationale and ingredients used for cures may be different but the goals remain the same. That is the true essence of Hoodoo and one you must grasp fully before you move on to the next chapter, "Getting Started With Hoodoo".

There you can learn more about the myths and legends surrounding the craft as well as the material used to create the charms, and other devices used as vessels for the supernatural to wield their power.

CHAPTER 3
GETTING STARTED WITH HOODOO

The authentication of Hoodoo in the 21st century has been questioned many times. In the previous chapter, you read about the interest young African-American Christians were showing in their heritage and in particular the craft of Hoodoo.

These people are desperately seeking sources to authenticate the factors that define this traditional North American folk magic.

They are navigating through the weeds of carefully sown seeds of doubt that portray Hoodoo as a taboo craft and a hoax, and a form of black magic that is best left alone.

That is a tough image to change.

Still, Hoodoo has existed and has even been

glamorized over the years, its true nature and power exalted by the many believers who today go beyond the Black-American society. But because of the commercialized image of Hoodoo, not everyone who claims to be a Hoodooist is a true one.

Only the people of African heritage are able to perform Hoodoo, due to their ability to call on the spirits of their oppressed ancestors the slaves whose deaths helped manifest the practice.

Getting started with Hoodoo requires you to learn the basics. You already explored its history and you know the craft is unique to the diverse North American culture.

Since Hoodoo is not a religion but a practice, a novice believer is able to get started with the craft in an almost "do it yourself" pattern where you start off by forming a connection with your African heritage—the spirits of your ancestors. You must also get familiar with how Hoodoo works. The rules, the material used, and the beliefs. Keep in mind that Hoodoo is not a craft that you can practice on the spur of the moment. You cannot cast a spell or tie root and expect it to work if you have not been following the general norms of the craft on a daily basis. Daily cleansing rituals and giving thanks to ancestors must be followed on a regular basis before you can ask the spirits and saints for help.

It is true Hoodoo is greatly commercialized, a concept that started with the urbanization of African-American communities around the 1920s and 1930s. This shift in status led to Hoodoo becoming a glitzy money-earning commodity. Authentic root workers were replaced by celebrity conjurers.

Previously handmade charms, gris bags, and mojo bags started to disappear, and in their place, ready-made charms, potions, powders, and talismans to serve every need started to appear in specialized shops that sold everything from love potions to hexes.

Therefore, to get started with Hoodoo, the true Hoodoo, the folk practice created as an amalgamation of the different ethnicities that formed a bond of suffering during the height of the North American slave trade, you must learn about the real tools and methods used by the conjure men and women born into slavehood on the great Southern plantations.

In this chapter you will learn about the workings of Hoodoo; learn about crossroads, spiritual baths, and working tricks with the aid of roots, crystals, and herbs. Hoodoo is not a craft that you can pick up on the spur of the moment, you cannot make a mojo bag from instructions online and expect it to work. You must know the significance of each ingredient put in that pouch, and how they interact with each other to create more power. You must build up your faith and convince the spirits, offer daily prayers to the ancestors, and confirm your intentions as a true believer; it is only then that you can step into the realm of Hoodoo conjure and expect the magic to work.

How Does Hoodoo Work? Spirits, Places, and Tools

Most newcomers to Hoodoo start off with a simple conjure, a ritual to manifest a blessing or initiate a simple change in their situation.

Hoodoo is popular not simply because it becomes a powerful and accessible tool for all believers, but for the benefits of practicing conjure, which you too can easily learn and master through daily rituals, faith and practice.

Hoodoo is often sought out for the following benefits.

- Protection—herbs, and roots are used to create mojo bags that can be worn for protection. Popular ingredients used to create protection mojo bags are basil and morning glory. The Angelica root too is a popular root for protection. It can be added to a mojo bag and hung around your neck or in a room to which you seek to offer protection. Make sure the mojo/Gris bag is not visible to anyone. If seen or touched by anyone other than the beneficiary of the bag, the charm will lose its power.

- Manifestation—Hoodoo is also popular for its power of manifestation. You can ask the spirits to grant your desires by manifesting them. Placing your intentions in an offering at a crossroads or inside a mojo bag will help you to reach your desires through the intercession of the spirits in the roots you use.

- Wealth and good luck—are other attractions of Hoodoo. You can practice creating mojo bags to attract luck with a combination of the following ingredients. John the Conqueror root, luck hand root, a rabbit's foot, and fast luck oil. Fast Luck Oil is very popular for attracting good fortune at gambling games, rubbing some oil on your lottery tickets, and even on Bingo cards. Sudden and fast windfalls are guaranteed when believers use the oil which is often a combination of olive oil and botanicals such as juniper, cinnamon, rose, fenugreek, etc.

Before Hoodoo was 'glamorized', rootworkers looked for their tools in nature.

Some examples of popular tools used include the John the Conqueror root, chewing John roots, black cat bones, five-finger grass, and devil's shoestring.

These tools of Hoodoo were blessed by the supernatural following rituals performed by the rootworkers. They were then handed over to the believers as talismans and mojo charms for obtaining desired goals.

Hoodoo beliefs too change from region to region, the reason being that in each part of the continent, the influences that shaped Hoodoo were different. The south, for example, home to slaves brought in from Angola and Congo, influenced Hoodoo practices with Western African beliefs.

The unique and slight differences in how a family practiced Hoodoo were passed down from generation to generation until the changes became a distinctive characteristic of a family's Hoodoo practice.

A Hoodoo conjurer uses various materials to manifest a spell. Animal parts, including bones, herbs, and other botanicals, and minerals such as salts and oils. Bodily fluids such as semen, menstrual blood, and urine are the most common when a spell is being performed for personal gain, distancing, or revenge.

The commonest reasons believers visit a rootworker/conjurer to obtain favors are centered on love, luck, money, revenge, divination, health, employment, and intimate relationship problems.

Modern-Day Hoodooism

A visit to the nearest spiritual shop will reveal to you a wonderful world of ready-made Hoodoo tools. Plus additional items such as color-coded candles with pre-cast spells, enchanted oils, and even sprays. They are far from the natural material the traditional conjurer picked up in the wild. Instead, these are synthetic substances made in factories supplying the modern Hoodoo industry. Likewise, there are people who practice the craft as a commercial commodity, most of these people are false Hoodooists (although some genuine Hoodooist will at times go on to benefit from their power). Hence, it is important to find a verified Hoodooist to further your interest in the craft.

None of those tools whether authentic or commercially bought will work if you cannot make a connection with the spirits of your ancestors, and to do so you must understand the rules of Hoodoo conjure.

While traditional Hoodooist offered believers their services through working tools gathered from scavenging the woods and fields, the modern believer can simply visit the nearest spiritual shop to pick up their supplies. The shops in turn receive stocks from manufacturers who supply them with their zoological and botanical charms. For either to work you must be a believer, make that important connection with your heritage and practice the craft within the parameters of balance.

The Rules and Parameters of Hoodoo Conjure

Conjures' primary goal is to initiate *change* or to manifest a change in the believer's situation. Sometimes a change is done through the manipulation of a circumstance.

Divination or reading-on a believer will help the root worker to define the problem. If the person seeking help is having problems the root worker can through divination find the source. Sometimes it turns out to be a hex put there by someone else, sometimes it could be a block of energy or closed doors at the crossroads of life.

Since Hoodoo is an amalgamation of the Christian religion, it is common practice to use *Psalms* from the Bible during a conjuring ritual. Therefore, it is not uncommon for rootworkers to be known as Catholics. This is common in predominantly Catholic areas such as South Carolina and New Orleans where rootworkers will even attend Sunday mass.

A fine example of the integration of Catholicism into Hoodoo conjure is the veneration of Catholic saints, the use of Catholic symbols during rituals, and the recital of psalms and prayers.

Many Hoodoo conjurers even call the Bible their book of spells. The Bible is often taken to the crossroads as a weapon of protection against the evil spirits that resided. Also, rootworkers are able to decipher the psalms to use as spells to offer cures for marital problems, simple headaches, and good luck for safe travel.

Often a rootworker working on a ritual to remove a hex put on a person will quote verses from the Bible to drive out the evil influence.

Christian similarities extend to the saints of Hoodoo too with many from the Christian religion being invoked through roots. Saint Expedite was a Roman soldier who was executed for his conversion to Christianity, and in Hoodoo he is venerated as a saint to grant speedy solutions to problems that cannot wait or to end any type of delay that may be causing problems for the believer. Expedite is also the saint for overcoming procrastination and he is portrayed stamping down on a crow because the caw-caw of a crow is supposed to symbolize the phrase tomorrow-tomorrow. These are only a few examples of the similarities Hoodoo shares with Christianity.

The Importance of Night and Day in Hoodoo

When practicing Hoodoo you will learn that the realms of night and day co-exist, as mirrors of each other—alternate realities.

Therefore the spirits have the power to influence how your life turns out through manifestation. An important aspect of Hoodoo's spiritualism is balance. You must learn to maintain a balance between both worlds. And when both realities become the same you can expect that change you desire.

You must also learn about the spirits in roots and the fundamentals that govern both the world of the living and the world of the dead. You must get a grasp of the positive and negative powers that a Hoodooist can wield. Remember that maintaining a balance between the elements of good and bad is important to work real magic through Hoodoo and enjoy its benefits.

The day is for the physical being in the general context of how we humans function.

Therefore, there is the daytime to supplement your physical body with energy, to do all the things you must to get on with your life. Daytime supplements and supports your activities—it is a time for living.

As nighttime approaches, you are physically fatigued as your natural bodily rhythm tells you it is time to prepare for rest. Therefore, in Hoodoo the night is not for the living, instead, it is the time when the veil between the spirit realm and the physical world is lifted. Therefore, nighttime is when the dead awaken. A time for spirits to enter the world of the living.

This concept is very significant in Cemetary Hoodoo where conjurers visit graveyards at night. You will learn more about that as we delve into aspects of cemetery Hoodoo.

The Right and Left Hand of Conjure

Remember I told you Hoodoo was all about 'balance', no matter how powerful a conjurer is they must always maintain a balance between good and bad. The Left and Right Hands of conjure exist to define that balance.

Right-Hand work refers to the conjurer's work to bring about prosperity, blessings, healings, a change of situation, and the opening of new doors leading to better prospects for believers. This work is achieved in combination with a spiritual connection to the ancestors, and the power of rootwork.

Examples of daily Right-Hand rituals you can indulge in include sweeping your house from the back to the front. You do this to drive out negativity and the influence of any evil your home may be under.

Another one is to make offerings at crossroads. The offering can be made by dropping a few coins at the crossroad; it is a good practice to have some change handy when traveling. This act appeases the spirits of the crossroads and in doing so you are making sure the doors of opportunity remain open to you.

Cleanse your spiritual aura by asking for protection from your Black-American ancestors. They can work to make sure spiritual influences remain good for you and any bad residue is removed.

Reciting psalms from the Bible is another way to guarantee blessings and protection for yourself. You can recite these prayers while sweeping your home as a cleansing ritual.

The Left Hand in Hoodoo refers to the use of the practice for causing damage, vengeance, and ill health, but not entirely in that context. Using Left Hand Hoodoo to cause mischief is often a result of reversing any mischief that has been caused to the seeker.

Let's say a person has been put under a curse by an enemy who wants to see his downfall. A rootworker upon reading the seeker's condition will be able to identify the type of hex put and will proceed to reverse the curse which is how Left Hand Hoodoo works. Reversing the curse and transferring it to the person who wished it on the seeker is often done as a form of justice and revenge. Therefore Left Hand work must not be classified as dark Hoodoo, it is merely taking care of business and ensuring the safety of the seeker.

Spiritual Cleansing

Cleansing is another aspect of Hoodoo you must learn about. Seeking a cure for illness or a bad situation, or influence in life can be overcome through the process of cleansing or spiritual baths. This practice is common in many cultures and countries across the world. In Hoodoo a series of cleansing baths are prescribed to be followed by the believer. Scented crystals are added to the water and offer various curative powers. You will find a range of scented crystals sold at spiritual stores for treating various situations.

To perform a spiritual cleansing the crystals are dissolved in a tub of water or pail which is then poured over the body. While doing so you can recite or try manifesting your desires and wishes or say a prayer or read a psalm from the Bible. Psalms 51 for cleansing and 91 for protection are often recited during a cleansing procedure.

Scented crystals are even used in mop water for cleansing the house of impurities and negative forces. Or as a magnet for attracting good luck and positive energy, the crystals will be dissolved and used to wash clothes.

The use of minerals in cleansing is one of the basic practices of Hoodoo and is a part of the African and European cultures adopted into the practice.

Running water is considered the purest form of water for cleansing; a fine example of how important cleansing is is the ritual of baptism started by John the Baptist who offered people deliverance from their sins through a cleanse in the River Jordan.

Minerals, roots, tree bark, salt, and herbs are often used as material for spiritual baths. If you are purchasing crystals from a spiritual store they will be labeled for different purposes.

Cleansing can be used for removing what is called 'foot track magic' in Hoodoo. A practice brought over by Hoodoo's African ancestors, the spell can be used for good or bad.

During the process of working this magic, a concoction of roots, grave dirt, etc. is laid across the path of the person you are working the magic on. Once trampled the magic enters their body and will start to manifest the desired results the foot track magic is expected to offer.

When foot track magic is used for evil, where

goopher dust is often a part of the ingredients, it has the power to bring negativity to the person's life and body.

Often when foot track magic is used against a person, it is with dark intentions, intended to bring about sickness and death, or crossing, hot-footing, and banishment.

A popular spell for attracting good luck and obtaining your goals is the Crown of Success Spell. People sitting for exams or having an important meeting or interview for a job they desire, seek out the power of this spell. Having a cleansing bath using Crown of Success oil will attract good luck and positivity.

Some popular crystals are those used for love potions and for protection. Here are the most used types of Hoodoo crystals.

- Pyrite—this stone is often added to a mojo bag or cleansing ritual as a means of attracting good luck and prosperity.

- Magnetite which is a type of naturally occurring magnet also called Lodestone—is a popular crystal for deflecting the evil eye. A Lodestone will offer protection from hexes and will even strengthen the power of other materials used in the spell.

- Black Tourmaline—offers protection, this stone is good for empowering a person with self-confidence. This stone will also help to negate the power of negative or evil energies aimed at you.

- Rose Quartz—pink is an important color in Hoodoo, and Rose Quartz is the main crystal used for love charms.

Understanding Root Work

To be successful in the craft and practice real Hoodoo, you must understand how to work a root, to do so you must make that all-important connection with the spirits of your ancestors; embrace your heritage.

Rootwork, where the entire plant is used for conjure, was created out of the belief that spirits reside in the trees, plants, animals, soil, rain, lightning, and minerals.

Roots connect you with the creator, therefore in Hoodoo, we believe that roots are a primal power, connecting us to the force that created the universe.

It is from where Hoodoo draws its power. These elements found in nature are your connection between the spirit world and the physical world. Spirits reside in the roots therefore, harnessing their power will help you to create a change by asking the spirits to work between realms and grant what you seek. Unlike the physical man, spirits are able to travel between realms, initiating change.

Each root has a specific spirit assigned to it. Each plant defined by its flowers, seeds, and roots will be used for specific purposes

You must open up a portal between the two realities, yours and the supernatural. When the spirits of a specific root you are using to obtain a favor, work on that need, there is a mirroring of that change between the two realms, making your desires a reality. Maybe to get a promotion in your job, win the love of someone, etc.

The spirits of the roots will work with you to open new pathways at the crossroads of life. These doorways which were blocked become open once you have begun to work with roots. Listed below are some popular roots used for performing various tricks.

Powerful Spirit Places

A spirited place in Hoodoo is a location where there is a convergence of spirits. The most favorable of these places are the spots where the residing spirits willingly work to aid the work of the conjurer. Some places will be more powerful than others if it is a kind of hub for conducting spiritual ceremonies.

For example, if a particular crossroad is often used as an altar by rootworkers, the number of good spirits dwelling there and willing to help increases. Hence, it becomes an almost sacred place for performing all sorts of Hoodoo rituals. Next, I will tell you about some of the most significant spirit places that are an important aspect of the craft.

Spirits

Before you begin seeking the help of spirits you must make an effort to understand the spirits. The closest spirits to you are those of your ancestors. I will explain further about making a connection with them. It is only once you have connected with the spirits of your ancestors must you reach out to other spirits.

These spirits are all around us. As I told you before, each root belongs to a certain spirit and you must get thoroughly familiar with the workings of a root before you try to harness its power. Spend time learning about roots, their parts, and their various functions.

You must develop a deep respect for these spirits, including those of your ancestors. Offering up daily prayers and gifts is the best way to honor them and show them your respect.

Always work with spirits on a basis of giving and take. Never take from a spirit without giving something in return. Because the gift or favor you were offered can just as easily be reversed. Now let's move on to the most powerful places to make contact with spirits.

The Crossroads

In Hoodoo, quite similar to most religions, crossroads are a place of power, a land that does not belong to any man or realm. Crossroads are an altar where offerings are made and new paths are opened.

There you will find a doorway between your world and that of the spirit. Understand that many spirits reside at crossroads. It is there that you follow your destiny or path in life by opening up blocks that are stopping you from reaching the goal you desire.

You will work with spirits on a basis of giving and taking.

You must make an offering—a gift—in return for the favor you ask. Keep in mind that the 'give-and-take' policy must be adhered to because spirits if not properly compensated will take back whatever favor it is they granted. Therefore, a visit to the crossroads must be made with a proper offering. A vessel containing a photo of yourself together with biological parts of your body such as a bit of hair, toenail, or fingernail clippings, as well as sugar, and red palm oil, are often added. This offering is then buried while performing traditional crossroad offerings which is to indulge in a smoke or a drink of whiskey.

For example, if you were to work on a Hoodoo love mojo, such as the "follow me boy spell" the blend of ingredients to create the root, and make the boy you desire return your affections, would need to be buried at every intersection/crossroad leading from your house to his.

If you are working a hex though such as a "crossing spell", the discarded material would be left in the cemetery. These hexes are created to turn good luck into bad, to induce spiritual hostility, and for vengeance. Other times the used tools would be thrown into running water, that is if you are working on a spell to get away from a situation.

Crossroads are also used to discard used tools. Burnt candle wax, water leftover from a ritual, ashes from burning incense, etc. This waste is thrown to a side of the crossroads, after which the believer walks away without looking back.

Conjurers learned to improvise, and where there was no easy access to a crossroad, an artificial one was created. A circle would be drawn with a large X inside indicating the four corners of the crossroad. This image would be called a cross-mark or even simply an 'X'. Scented powders called *sachet (sashay) powders* are used to draw the cross, either on the floor or on a made-up altar. I will explain more about Hoodoo powders in chapter three.

Sometimes the mark would be totally invisible and indicated with just five dots to symbolize the four roads and meeting points. This type of made-up crossroad would not be called the X. Instead, you will hear the names five-spot, cosmogram, or quincunx. The five-spot crossroad will not be used for disposing of spells, it serves more as an altar for *fixing spells*.

Offerings will be kept on each 'dot'; the type of objects placed on the dots will depend on the spell.

The main point to understand when it comes to the crossroads alter is that it is one of the vessels through which you will be able to manifest the power of roots enabling you to make a connection and harness the power of change by connecting the physical and spiritual world.

Cemetery Hoodoo, Graveyard Spirits, and Working Tricks

The type of spirits present at a cemetery are varied, plus, the potency of a graveyard is considered to be very high when seeking to perform a Hoodoo trick. Cemetery Hoodoo can be practiced for good and for bad; remember that Left-Hand Hoodoo must be used for the greater good only, as a defense, retaliation, and getting back at someone but never as a way of merely performing black magic with evil intent. Therefore, cemetery Hoodoo must be performed with that all-important 'balance' in mind.

Cemetery conjure can be practiced for blessings or for invoking a terrible curse on someone. However to do either you must first gain experience on how Hoodoo functions, more importantly, develop an open relationship with the spirits.

Graveyards function on many different levels in Hoodoo.

- They are the burial grounds for your ancestors and a good place to create a connection and offer prayers as part of connecting with your heritage.

- A cemetery is a place where you can find a crossroad to set up an altar to make your offerings to the spirits.

- It is home to many different types of spirits, from different backgrounds and different religions coexisting. Therefore, it is a good place to make your spiritual connection.

A cemetery is a place of open principles in the sense that it is a place devoid of labels. Religion, race, or social standing in life do not matter there, the only common factor is death. Death is inevitable for us all and therefore, not to be feared. Keep this factor in mind and you will be able to make strong connections with the spirits of the graveyard.

Graveyards represent a place of rest, a hub of tranquility that is not affected by the chaos of the modern world. Hence it is a place of reflection for you to find solitude and peace to practice the craft. A cemetery will give you more access to spirits than any other place, it is a marvelous meeting point for the dead and the living to connect. It is also a station through which other spirits will pass through, giving you a chance to make a connection with spirits and entities of different levels. Think of a cemetery as a symbolic gateway. A point from which the living and the dead can cross interconnect.

Graveyard dirt is a potent ingredient for use in spells and is an important ingredient for making Goofer dust. It is particularly powerful when used for creating counter curses or reversing work done to you by another party.

When gathering cemetery dirt it is important to have a deep spiritual connection with the spirit giving you the dirt. Through the cemetery soil, the spirit will gain direct access to you and the work you are performing, therefore, it is important to make a proper connection and understand the nature of the spirit you are dealing with. Ensuring you develop a healthy connection with the spirit you are dealing with is important for the success of your work and will decide whether the work you perform turns out to be positive or negative.

You must perceive a cemetery as follows.

- A place of rest and tranquility for the dead and the living.

- A place to communicate with the dead

- A place to work

In Hoodoo we consider the cemetery, crossroads, and places of flowing water to be the most potent, powerful places. Graveyards have been blessed with prayer, they are sanctified grounds where the dead can lay at rest. To access the spirits there you must learn to listen, it is only then that you will begin to realize that the spirits have been talking to you all this time. To start your graveyard work you must first lay the groundwork. Introduce yourself to the spirits and let them judge you and decide for themselves (because the spirits are very similar to living in that aspect) whether they like you or not.

Therefore, it is important to follow certain etiquette when visiting a cemetery.

- Start to make regular visits to the cemetery as a sort of introduction. But never visit empty-handed. That is rude. You must appease the gatekeeper, typically the spirit from the first grave you encounter at the entrance.

- Take along an offering that you can drop at the entrance. A sort of gift for the doorman. Traditional offerings include candy, whiskey, cigars, cigarettes, baked goods, apples, herbs (make sure not to include ingredients used in banishment spells), and of course the all-time favorite coins; they are goodies rootworkers have identified as favorites the spirits enjoy.

- Try to find gravesites that are over 100 years or close to it. Graves that have not been disturbed for long periods of time are best to conduct your work at, as it is rude to disturb recent graves, which will in turn upset the loved ones of the person buried there.

- You must never take anything out of the cemetery until the spirits have given you permission to do so. The cemetery is a very humbling place, therefore make sure to pay the highest respect to the spirits there as you are seeking their help and not vice-versa.

Once you have made your entrance offering you can walk into the cemetery. Often a rootworker will shield their faces when entering a cemetery because, as you know spirits talk, and if there is a conjurer already working with spirits in that particular cemetery, chances are your visit could be revealed to them if the spirits recognize you; Hoodoo magic works best when shielded from outsiders, therefore try your best to keep your identity hidden from spirits you are not working with.

A common practice when entering the graveyard is to walk in backward or have a cloth thrown across the face, even your palms acting as a shield will do. This is merely to shield your identity from the spirits who may be having a working connection with other conjurers from revealing your presence to them. It is therefore a practice reserved for only when you visit the graveyard for conjure work and not for when you are attending a funeral. Once your work at the cemetery is done do not leave without offering a gracious "thank you" to the spirits.

Leave your work when done and walk away without a backward glance, this gesture establishes trust; trust that your work is going to be successful. Remember Lot's wife, from the book of Genesis in the Bible, who turned into a pillar of salt as she looked back at Sodom and Gomorrah as they burned. Looking back symbolizes doubt, be strong and believe in yourself for the magic to work.

How to Make a Connection With Spirits— Divination

The closest and strongest relationship you will develop among the spirits will be the ones you form with your ancestors. They are family and will be your best allies helping you to carry out your conjure work. But make sure to appease your ancestors, as I told you before, the practice of Hoodoo begins with laying the groundwork, and starting with ancestor veneration on a daily basis is important for you to develop credibility as a rootworker, among your ancestors and the spirit world. Remember this tie is the most important in rootwork. If you recall I explained to you how every part of a root is inhabited by a specific spirit, therefore the strength of your spiritual connection will be the key to your success.

Keep in mind the cemetery can be dangerous if you are a novice, and trying to dabble with the spirit world in a cemetery before you are properly experienced can lead to you becoming the victim of a malicious spirit.

Therefore, the safest voyage into the spirit world as a rookie Hoodooist is to start making a connection with your ancestor's spirits.

Establish an altar to them, nothing elaborate is needed; a candle, a few pictures if you have them and a bowl of water will be fine. Add the names of your dear departed relatives on a piece of paper to the altar. You can make daily offerings of candy, alcohol, or any of their favorite food.

Light the candle and offer daily blessings to your ancestors, talk to them and listen; through consistency and patience, you will be able to make a connection. It is a timely process, but eventually, you will make a connection.

Physically hearing them may take time, instead, you will feel certain vibes, and develop sudden cravings for food or alcohol which is how your ancestors let you know what they want. You may be able to see them in your dreams and talk to them. And eventually, you *will* begin to physically hear their voices—it is quite a shock at first, but remain calm and you will soon become familiar with their voices. Once you establish a strong connection with the spirits of your ancestors, you can visit the cemetery to broaden your experience of connecting with spirits of different temperaments, characteristics, wisdom, and also intent, which can be good or bad.

Spirits of the Cemetery

Do not expect to make a connection with a spirit on your first visit to the cemetery. You must first introduce yourself and allow the spirits to evaluate you. Some may be interested and some may just ignore you altogether, while others may try to trick you into gaining from you with no intention of returning any favors.

Absorb the solitude of the place and teach yourself to sense and listen. Walk around pausing around the graves, see if you feel a vibe, if you don't move on and if you do hang around longer to make sure you feel a connection. Once you do establish a feeling that connects you to the grave, observe the names on the tombstone. Take your information home and try to find out what you can about the people buried there. Knowing, if possible, their nature and character when they were alive will help you to establish if the spirit calling out to you has good intentions or bad.

In time you are bound to make a stronger connection with a spirit who is interested in getting to know you better and helping you with your work.

Open your mind and senses so you can feel the spirit trying to communicate with you. Get in tune with the vibes; if you feel fear, or dread it is best not to make a connection with that spirit; otherwise, feelings of joy or positivity will indicate a good spirit that is trying to communicate with you. Keeping yourself sensitive to these vibes is important to establish a proper connection.

Once you make the connection, treat your new friendship like any other. Start by getting acquainted with your new spirit friend. Do not get down to business immediately. That is rude. Plus, you can't go around asking spirits you barely know for favors.

Taking along the usual offerings will help seal the friendship, as you start to discover more about your spirit friend. Cultivate that friendship just as you would one with a living person, and plan regular meetings to keep the connection. Once you feel you have built a solid relationship and you are assured of the spirit's intentions to help, you can ask them for help with some of your work.

Precautions to Follow at a Cemetary— Cleansing Rituals, Take Back No Parasites

As described above your experience at the cemetery is not going to be an all rosy-cozy relationship with a kind spirit. There are many dangers to heed.

One important factor to keep in mind is to be consistent. You may have to make many visits to the graveyard, and take along many offerings or gifts before you even begin to make a connection with a spirit there.

Don't let the excitement of finally making a connection with the spirit world blind you to the dangers. Not all spirits are good, and some will try to trick you and cause harm. One way to discern the nature of spirits is to be attuned to the vibes you get off them, as I said before if you feel dread, anger or fear leave those spirits alone, but sometimes those spirits may not leave you alone.

There are malicious spirits who are hungry for a change of scene, they are looking for a free ride and you would look like the perfect vessel to walk out of the cemetery in. You can prevent an unwelcome spirit from latching onto you by performing a cleansing ritual.

In the section on cleansing, you learned about using crystal powder in baths as a form of spiritual cleansing. That is exactly what you must practice following a visit to the graveyard.

- You could take home, unknowingly, a parasitic spirit that has attached itself to you. This spirit will feed off your power and cause all sorts of problems. A cleansing ritual after leaving the cemetery will ensure this does not happen.

- You may have accidentally messed with some other rootworkers' work. Therefore, you could fall victim to whatever the intention of that work was. Again a cleansing ritual on leaving the cemetery will ensure the work does not manifest itself in you.

- Do not enter the cemetery to conduct your work decked up in any jewelry that can fall off. Leaving behind your personal effects will give spirits access to you, as they can form a connection with you through the jewelry.

- Do not wear open-toe shoes or any type of footwear that will cause graveyard dirt to be tracked back to your home. That dirt in your home will become a portal for an evil spirit to follow you back.

- Likewise, it is customary to cover your head when entering the cemetery, now I told you to do this to avoid recognition, but covering your head serves another purpose, the head is believed to be a gateway into your body, and when left exposed a spirit can use it to enter. Additionally, you can rub some Florida Water on your forehead to act as a protective barrier.

A temporary cleanse can be done once you leave the cemetery to be followed by a proper spiritual cleanse once you get home. Florida Water is effective when mixed with salt crystals. You can rub the mix from your head to your toes cleansing yourself and pushing out any unwelcome presence that may have latched on to you.

Once home, you can use the same ingredients added to a tub of bathwater or in a bucket which you can use to pour over your head, thus washing out the negativities.

What is Florida Water?

It is neither water nor does it come from Florida. This liquid is a kind of mildly scented cologne made from a base of alcohol. In the olden days, citrus and lavender were the main scents used, although the ingredients will vary in Florida Water made today. The name Florida is a derivation of the Spanish word *florido* which means 'floral' probably as an indication of what the contents smell. Florida water is often used for protection and for attracting good luck to yourself as well as your home or place of work.

Harnessing the Power of the Cemetery

The power that you will find in a cemetery is turbulent, it can veer between both positive and negative energies. That is why you must only approach graveyard conjuring once you have gained some experience in conversing and dealing with spirits and after you have increased your knowledge of Hoodoo and how best to protect yourself or block unwelcome forces.

The type of vibe you feel at the cemetery will differ from grave to grave. The power emanating from the grave of a person who met a violent or suffering death will be different from that of some who lived content and happy life. There are frustrations, anger, sadness, evil, and boredom to deal with when attempting to get the help of cemetery spirits.

Some spirits will agree to help you with your rootwork to bring about good luck, protection and wealth, etc. While some spirits will eagerly assist you with casting a lethal curse on someone.

Becoming a seasoned conjurer who can navigate the cemetery takes a lot of time and practice, therefore don't be in a hurry to practice conjuring at the graveyard because getting your work wrong can have dire consequences.

You can, however, harness the immense wealth of knowledge found at a graveyard. The place is home to spirits from all walks of life, people who have dealt with all types of situations in life, and ghosts who have learned more in death. Therefore, you have access to an immeasurable amount of knowledge that you can learn to harness to improve your life and help others. One of the most potent ingredients to take out of a cemetery is dirt from a grave. This root is full of potent power and can help enhance the work you are doing together with the combined help of the spirit from whose grave you took the dirt.

Manifesting a Love Spell With Graveyard Dirt

This is a simple trick to work, you will need Valerian root as well as dirt from the grave of a person who showed you affection. Mix the two ingredients together and find a way to sprinkle the powder on the personal belongings of the person you love; clothes, or shoes are ideal.

Protection for Your Home

You will need dirt from the grave of a spirit you have a good relationship with. Take that dirt and combine it with equal amounts of salt which you must then sprinkle around the windows and doorways, as well as the surroundings of your home to create a powerful barrier of protection.

Drive Away an Enemy

The spell you create to drive away someone with graveyard dirt is a lot more potent than when you use the Hot Foot Powder. You will need to collect dirt from the grave of an unprincipled person. Collect the dirt from where the heart would be, and mix the soil with sulfur and red pepper. You can tie it up in a red pouch and bury that mojo bag in a corner of the person's garden, make sure to choose the eastern edge to do so.

Using graveyard dirt to drive away someone is a very strong spell. Because of the strong power found within a cemetery, the spell can cause incredible harm to the person, in addition to driving them away, therefore, keep in mind the rules of Hoodoo and maintain a balance when practicing Left-Hand work. Revenge should only be sought out when absolutely necessary and justified.

Create a Mojo Hand of Prosperity

You will need to find the grave of a person who was prosperous in life. Quite often a conjurer will seek out the grave of someone who was a successful businessman, or a banker. The most important work of this spell is establishing a relationship with the spirit of the chosen person. Remember you need the permission of the grave's spirit to take away the dirt. The spell works in combination with other ingredients.

- Orange peel symbolizes prosperity.

- Cloves or black-eyed peas symbolize luck and new pathways.

- Fingernail clippings

- Pennies and silver coins

Add everything to a small pouch and ask for permission from the spirit to carry out your work, once you receive it, dig a hole and put in the coins. You can pour in some whiskey as an offering too, as a way to sweeten the deal. Then drop in the bag and close up the hole. Dig it out after seven days and you can then wear the mojo bag like a magnet for good luck blessed by the spirits of the dead. When digging up the hand make sure to give the spirit there another gift.

Hoodoo Dirt

Conjure draws its power from the Earth. The trees, the leaves, animals, water, and dirt. Grounding all this and creating a connection is the soil of the land—dirt. Therefore, in Hoodoo dirt holds immense power. It is where the dead are buried and therefore contains the power of the spirits.

Dirt is from where new life sprouts; rivers, and streams make their way through paths created by dirt, it is the foundation on which we build our homes, and the ground on which we grow our food.

The earth contains within it the cycle of life from birth to death and is the most powerful tool in conjure absorbing the power of the living and spiritual world. The earth beneath our feet connects us to all other tools—the crossroads, roots, and graveyard.

In Hoodoo we believe that our ancestors empower the earth. Their bodies have decayed and become one with the land from which new life springs. Therefore, they live again in the trees, plants, and water. Therefore the dirt of your land is your divine connection to your heritage.

You too will return to feed the earth just as your ancestors do therefore the power of the earth is boundless. And harnessing that power whether it is graveyard dirt or dirt from a crossroad, or your own backyard, you are using the essence of your ancestors to work your conjure.

CHAPTER 4
MATERIAL USED IN HOODOO

You have learned about places, spirits, and roots. In addition to these important aspects of Hoodoo, there are staple tools that every root worker must have around. These ingredients must always be a part of your stock as they play an important role in just about every work.

In this chapter, you will learn about the important material used in Hoodoo Conjure. The significance of each tool and how they influence your work.

Hoodoo Candles

The staple of all tools used when working on a trick is the candle. It is the beacon of light that paves the way for the rest of the work to be done.

In Hoodoo the candle represents light and an illuminated path. It is a guide to show you the way, enlightening your path to guide you in the right direction.

Candles can be fixed to work a certain spell or they can be lit as an offering to the spirits. Candles have been used in ancient religions since the beginning. Candles have represented spiritual and magical beliefs in Roman, Egyptian, and Mediterranean cultures.

Candles are often one of the chosen tools among beginner Hoodooists. There are many tricks to be performed with candles, plus they are cheap; making them the ideal choice for learners.

A candle in Hoodoo serves many purposes; it can be used to illuminate the path for those seeking a special favor or the help of a spirit, it can be used to get rid of or burn obstacles and it can be used for casting spells.

While a seasoned rootworker will dress and fix candles with magical ingredients, to serve a specific purpose, you can easily purchase pre-loaded candles from your spiritual shop. Pre-loaded candles are those which have been imbibed with the power of enchanted oils, roots, and herbs.

In Hoodoo we use candles for many reasons, you can burn a candle with an intention attached to it, and as that candle burns your needs are communicated to the universe. In other words, your requests are sent across to the realm of the spirit world. The roots used to dress the candles will let the spirits know your desires so they can set about manifesting what you seek.

Candles are also used as offerings to spirits. They appease the spirit's appetite by feeding it smoke and light which spirits desire.

The popularity of candles only increased after the end of the Civil War, before that slaves did not have access to them as they were expensive, used only on the big plantations and slaves only had access to lanterns as a means of illumination. However, once African-Americans started to move to urban areas, Hoodoo took a turn and as you already learned, opened up a huge market of commercially produced Hoodoo tools. This is when candles received a huge boost. There were color-coded candles and enchanted candles to choose from. Candles that are already fixed to perform a required task are available at spiritual shops for you to purchase, making them the easiest Hoodoo tool to try and master.

Terms Given to Hoodoo Candles

Before you visit a spiritual shop to purchase candles you must know the terminology attached to them.

- Fixed Candles

A fixed candle is one that has been dressed with roots and oils as well as blessed with prayers and intentions. Fixed candles are larger than the average type of Hoodoo candle and will come in a glass case. The candle's function will be printed on the front making it easy for you to choose. For example, the Money Draw candle will have its purpose displayed on the front and all you are required to do is light the candle at an altar and offer up prayers.

- Dressed Candles

Very similar to the Fixed Candle, this one means that the candle has been dressed with a specific root and oil to manifest what you desire. For example, if you are looking for a windfall and change in your monetary situation the candle can be 'dressed' with some Money Draw oil to manifest your desires. Since this candle is only 'dressed' you will have to 'fix' with prayers and intention when performing your ritual.

- Loaded Candles

They are just as the name suggests, loaded. The candles are hollowed out to facilitate oils and roots which can be thrust directly into the wax. The potency of the candle is believed to increase this way. If you are considering loading a candle thus, make sure to pick up a thicker stemmed candle so it does not crack.

- Rolled Candles

A candle that has been rolled in special oils and then in herbs is called a rolled candle. They are similar to the loaded candle, except the roots are stuck to the outside of the candle.

The Meaning of Colored Candles

Colored candles are not a part of Hoodoo culture. At the start candles were not even accessible to the slaves, leave alone color-coded ones. Simple candles were used and they were dressed with the intention of the rootworker.

However, we do live in modern times with candles freely available and in a variety of hues. Therefore, modern Hoodooist, and especially beginners like you will find that color-coded candles are very useful for staying focused on your intentions.

Color Coding for Candles

- Black candles—burn this when working a

protection spell or when you are fixing a hex on someone.

- White candles—although used for healing and obtaining blessings, a white candle can be used for performing any kind of conjure because white is neutral and the first type of candle used by your ancestors for performing Hoodoo magic. You can dress the candle with your intentions.

- Pink candles—in Hoodoo pink symbolizes love. Burn a pink candle for happiness in your home and for spiritual healing.

- Red candles—this is a powerful color and represents your lifeblood. A red candle will be used for manifesting strength and courage, as well as for intentions such as love and attraction.

- Orange candles—represent success, energy, and clarity.

- Green candles—this candle is lit with the intention of wealth and good luck. If you are seeking success in your job or future career offering your intentions through a lit green candle will help.

- Gold/Yellow candles—this candle is lit when a sudden change is desired. It is also lit for drawing good fortune.

- Blue candles—the power of this candle is a reflection of its tranquil color. Light one when you are trying to manifest joy, peace, happiness, and harmony within your life or home.

- Gray/Silver candles—they are lit for protection, or when you are working to banish an evil influence.

- Purple candles—to take control of a situation, maybe to turn tables at work or in your life.

- Brown candles—are quite appropriately colored, they are lit when seeking to win a court case.

You will also come across candles that have two colors. They are specially lit when you are working to reverse a particular situation.

- Black and white candles—these can be lit when you are working to reverse a curse/hex that has been put on you.

- Red and black candles—light one when you are working to reverse the evil influence of a person or spirit over your life.

- Green and black candles—are lit when you are working to reverse the financial difficulties that you are under.

- Red, white and green candles—offer triple blessings. When lit they offer you luck to draw money toward you, find love, and get rid of evil influences in your life.

Reading the Candle Flames

Reading a candle as it burns is something seasoned conjurers are able to do, it is not easy as the physical properties of a candle will change. How fast it burns, etc. depends on the quality of the candle.

The flame of a candle can be interpreted in the following manner.

- A flame that jumps up and down—if you see this in the candle you have lit, it could indicate the presence of spirits who are trying to reach out to you. A jumping flame could also indicate a warning. Deciphering the meaning will depend on your interpretation and intuition given to the situation you lit the candle for.

- A steady flame—when the flame burns tall and unmoving it is an indication the magic you are working on is going ahead as planned.

- A dancing flame—this is when the flames move around, back and forth in all directions. It is an indication of good energy but that energy is not focused. When you see this, you must try making your intentions clear to the spirit the candle represents.

- Tall flame—when you see the flame rise up it is an indication of good energy and that your intentions are going to manifest real soon. However, a tall flame also indicates that those fast achieved results will not last long.

- A small flame—indicates the energy flow is limited and your work will take longer to achieve. You can try refocusing and making your intention clearer.

- A blue flame—you will see the blue at the bottom of the flame, and it indicates your work is going to yield positive results.

- A crackling, popping, or a hissing flame— of course, this means only one thing, you have spirits that are trying to contact you.

- A green flame—if you see this then expect prosperity, especially if your intentions are for luck, success, and wealth.

- Black smoke puffs coming from the flame—is a sign that you have someone doing rootwork against you, it could mean you are under the influence of a spirit or conjurer.

- White puffs of smoke—will tell you that the work you are doing is progressing well.

Getting Started With Candle Work

Candles are a good first to start your work on Hoodoo conjure. They are cheap and you don't necessarily have to dress the candle, so you don't have to run out and purchase Hoodoo conjure oils. You can use a normal white candle for this purpose.

Start by holding the candle in both your hands and praying very clearly for your intention. Focus and think of the change you want and its outcome. Let's say you desperately want a promotion in your workplace. Make that intention clear, imagine getting that promotion and the positive change it will bring into your life. Focus on how you will be given the promotion, recognition of the productive work you have been doing, the salary increment that will be offered to compensate for the promotion, and the contributions you are making at your workplace.

Once you have made your intention clear to the spirits, (and not the candle, it is merely the vessel of transfer) place it in a safe place and light the candle. Stare into the flame and again make your intention very clear. Remember you are communicating to the spirits, and it is important to let them know the change you desire. Once you have made your intention clear, you can clear your mind and let the candle burn down.

Once it has burned down it indicates the transfer of your intention from the physical world to the spirit world where the spirits can get to work manifesting your desires.

Newcomers should start candle work simply. If you wish to dress or fix your candle, don't go out and buy a ready-made one. Purchase the Hoodoo conjure oils and roots and dress the candle yourself, ensuring you have a deeper spiritual connection to the entire work.

Water and Important Conduit in Hoodoo

In Hoodoo water plays an important part, it is the path that helps the spirits travel—the conduit. Placing a glass of water on the altar as you pray to the spirits will act as a doorway through which the spirits are able to enter the physical world. Therefore water is always present in a ritual.

Water is also the made ingredient for cleansing spells, it holds the power to wash away and cleanse you of any unwelcome influences. In spiritual practices, water symbolizes new beginnings, healing, and energy.

Rivers in Hoodoo are highly symbolic. They are places where many spirits reside and are important meeting places, similar to crossroads. It is a place of renewal, a vessel through which you can get rid of evil influences and perform cleansing rituals. The river can be used to renew your soul and indicates new beginnings. Baptisms are performed in rivers so the person receiving a cleanse can wash away their impurities and those impurities are then taken away by the flowing water.

Roots

Roots are another important material in Hoodoo and should be kept on hand to conduct your work. While you can purchase roots from a spiritual shop, you will also find many growing around your home and in the woods. Roots can be stored and dried in bunches, in jars, and as powders. Different roots have different effects and depend on the spirit that dwells within them.

The Devil's Shoestring

Among all the interesting names Hoodoo has awarded to roots, the Devil's Shoestring is probably the most appropriate. This root is a staple in protection spells as well as conjure work to invoke good luck.

Using the Devil's Shoestring is used to trip up the devil and evil work. Three types of roots belonging to the Honeysuckle plant genre (also a powerful plant used for binding spells) are used to make this root. It is widely believed that the Devil's Shoestring is a root the African slaves picked up from the native Red Indians who were held as slaves together with the people of Africa.

The three types of plans from which the roots are obtained include:

- Viburnum Alnifolium also called Hobble Bush found in Canada and the northern parts of the US.

- Viburnum Opulus, better known as the American Cranberry Bush although it is not really a type of cranberry. This plant too grows in the north and in Canada.

- Viburnum Prunifolium, popularly called Blackhaw. This is the only variety of Devils Shoestring which can be found growing in the southern states of the US and is therefore believed to be the original Devils Shoestring used by the slaves on the Southern plantations.

All three plants have long, flexible, and tangled-up roots making them perfect for tripping up evil. Learn about its uses in mojo bags as good luck spells that you can have when seeking wealth and advancement in your workplace.

There are many other types of plants too which are available under the same name, and often used for conjure work such as Devil's Shoestring. But ask any seasoned rootworker and they will tell you to not deviate from the original list of plants given above if you expect positive results.

Roots and Their Power

The number of roots and botanicals used in Hoodoo is wide. Each root serving a specific need will have the power to influence unique situations.

The Calamus Root

This influential root is also called Sweet Flag. A rootworker will offer this charm to a believer who seeks to gain control over a particular situation or even a person. Therefore, the Calamus root is often used in spells created for empowerment. Examples include the Follow Me Boy spell, commanding spells, and commanding spells. Calamus roots are used in conjure bags with a mix of other potent ingredients in case someone wishes to dominate or take control of a situation. Likewise, the root chips can be dried and burnt as incense when charming other talismans such as candles.

The Angelica Root

This powerful root has many names; the Archangel Root, Holy Ghost Root, and Dong Quai. The Angelica root is used in conjuring to empower women and as a protector and tool for healing. It is also a good luck charm for households and when dealing with health issues; the root is also believed to ward off evil influences. Placing the root in different colored pouches and combining it with various ingredients such as oils and flowers will offer diverse results.

High John the Conqueror Root

This is one of the main roots used by conjurers for working tricks. The High John the Conqueror root is used for manifesting all sorts of situations. Its main power lies in the ability to manipulate your luck, improve your love life, and for purposes of justice. In the olden days, the John the Conqueror root was worn by slaves seeking protection from the slave minders. High John the Conqueror Root was a symbol of power for the African slaves who used it to fight back, there are several stories that lead to the background of the root centered on a cunning slave a trickster who managed to manipulate his slow-minded masters.

Today, you can buy the root packaged according to size, there are even male and female roots you can decide to use depending on the type of trick you are planning on working on. The root can be worn whole on your body or added to mojo bags; it is available to buy whole, or as chips, powder, and oil. John the Conqueror Root, High John the Conqueror, Low John the Conker, and High John are some of the names the root is associated with.

Salep Root/Helping Hand Root/Lucky Hand Root

This root is carried by people seeking luck in gambling and games. Working the roots magic will yield good luck and fortunes. Therefore, it is often carried in a mojo bag by people seeking luck in games of chance. The name helping hand is a suggestion of how the root works—helping people who require sleight of hand to garner winning. Combine an entire Helping Hand Root with Five Finger Grass inside a red-colored flannel bag to attract money.

Five Finger Grass

Also called Cincoenrama or Cinquefoil, Five Finger Grass is a type of herb. In Hoodoo the plant is used for its magical powers. The five points of the leaf represent wisdom, love, money, health, and power. The herb is added to mojo bags or burned to invoke good luck and improve self-confidence.

Various parts of the plant are used for its curative powers against fever and diarrhea. In Hoodoo the herb is used for success, to empower your hands to work magic to bring you luck. The root is also used to manipulate others to come to your aid.

Dixie John Root

Another name for this root is Southern John or Beth Root. In Hoodoo conjure this root invokes blessings for prosperous family life, and improves one's sexual relationship and love. The root can be boiled and drunk as tea for improving your love life or added to the wash cycle of your bed sheets if you seek an improvement in your sex life.

Valerian Root

Also called Vandal Root is used at times as a replacement for graveyard dirt. It is a potent ingredient for manifesting peace within one's home, subduing quarrels, and also for darker tricks such as summoning demons.

Personal Material for Creating a Link

In Hoodoo working a change calls for your intentions to be clearly communicated. And in the case of a personal spell you are working on for yourself, another, or even a group of people, it is important to establish a strong and clear connection to the individual.

To establish this connection you will need to include personal effects. Popular material used for this purpose includes blood, sometimes menstrual blood, semen, worn and unwashed clothing, nail clippings, and bits of hair. By adding these personal items to your conjure work, you are including the essence of that individual in the work.

Additional material to establish the link can include a photograph and the full name of the person you are doing the conjure work on written on a piece of paper. Sometimes you may only have the name and a photograph to work with, keep in mind that working with these materials will not have as strong a connection as the personal items mentioned above.

Hoodoo Powders

The use of powders in Hoodoo is very much a part of the craft's Southern heritage. Blowing powder and sprinkling powder as a means of dispelling evil spirits, cleansing a place, and bringing in luck are practiced by several folk religions across the globe.

The use of blowing powders for powerful conjure work in the West Indies is common. Even in Asian nations such as the island of Sri Lanka, where the worship of the deities from nature is common, a traditional 'kattadiya' the local equivalent to rootworkers, will perform exorcisms or cures using smoke from burnt roots, drum beats, and the blowing of blessed powders in the face of victims to drive out demons.

There are many traditions Hoodoo conjurers followed in southern states, one is the sprinkling of blessed powder along the front step and in the four corners of one's house to keep out evil influences. Powders can be added to mojo bags to create good luck charms attracting love, money, good health, and power. Otherwise, powders can be added to dresser drawers to keep your clothes smelling good and for empowering the wearer with good luck.

Hoodoo powders are used in hexes and curse work too. Some can be used to drive a person away while others thrown on the doorstep or in the garden on one's enemy can attract bad luck to them and cause serious harm if the root worker so wishes.

The tradition of using powders in hoodoos is an old one, with roots in African, and European traditions. Towards the latter parts of the 19th century, the types of Conjure powder used began to change with scented powders offering various solutions for problems and being sold at spiritual stores. The powders are available as blowing and sprinkling *sashay* powders.

In the olden days though, before the

commercialization of Hoodoo, powders were made with a mix of herbs, roots, and minerals. They remain among the most popular in use today.

- Magnetic Sand

This powder which is an extremely fine iron grit which is a powdered form of cast iron shot is meant to act as a magnet drawing luck to you. Therefore, it is popular among people seeking winnings in games of chance, those wanting to increase their finances, and for luck in love.

A powerful combination for using Magnetic Sand is to attach it to a Lodestone —explained in chapter 2. The general practice is to get hold of two Lodestones. One is perceived as male and one as female. You then sprinkle the magnetic sand on the stones, which is called *feeding the he* and *feeding the she*. Carrying these stones around in a small velvet mojo bag will attract money as well as luck in love.

- Sulfur Powder

Sulfur was a popular material used by rootworkers in the olden days for work against an enemy, known as Enemy Tricks. It is a type of naturally occurring mineral dust that is used in several tricks. A popular one is when the sulfur powder is mixed with salt and laid out in lines as a form of cleansing for a house. Or when it is sprinkled in a cross from across the footprint of an enemy.

- Salt powder

Salt has been a versatile and necessary mineral in Hoodoo conjure from the beginning. It is often used for purification rituals, blessings, and for protection from magical influences. Inherited from European folk religions is the practice of placing a pinch of salt in every corner of the room before the commencement of the ritual.

Salt can be added to red pepper, or sulfur if you are working on a particularly potent spell against your enemy, but if it is simple protection, just salt alone will work. The type of salt whether sea salt, table salt, or kosher salt doesn't really make a difference.

- Red pepper powder

A vital ingredient used by rootworkers working on Enemy Tricks, red pepper is often an ingredient in Hot Foot Powder, Goopher Dust, and Crossing Powder.

- Black pepper powder

Works similar to red pepper powder and will be used in creating trouble for an enemy in the areas of family, job, and finances. Another way to cause mischief for an enemy is to add a personal/biological part of the person you are jinxing to a bottle containing red pepper powder, black pepper powder, salt, and sulfur. Bury the bottle at the entrance of your enemy's front door so they walk over it on a daily basis.

With the commercialization of Hoodoo, close to the 20th century, powders were ready-made and available in spiritual stores. Some were mixed with talcum powder and emitted a pleasant fragrance so people would dab them on their person.

Popular ready-made powder mixes include hot foot powder, the Crown of Success spiritual powder, King Solomon Wisdom powder, Crossing Powder and look me over powder.

How to Use Hoodoo Powder

A very traditional method of sprinkling powder is to do so while walking backward. It is customary to take an odd number of steps backward. Ideally, 21–steps if you have the room, or anywhere between three and nine will suffice.

Other methods of sprinkling Hoodoo powder

include:

- Blowing the dust in the direction of the person's house.

- Adding lines of small mounds of dust in corners of the house.

- Making a crossing pattern on the street for the enemy to walk over.

- Dressing candles with powder

- Dusting the powder on the personal items of the person you are working the trick on. Clothes, shoes, socks, and hankies are good choices.

- Blowing the powder in the four directions.

Dressing Items with Sachet/Sashay Powder

Dressing a candle with powder is often done once the candle has already been dressed with magic oil. A dab of oil over the powder is applied to create a potent dressing of double layers which some rootworkers believe increases the power of the candle.

You can also "dress paper" if they are important documents. When getting ready to send off any important documents out of which you are expecting favorable replies or outcomes, dress the paper with a dash of the crown of success powder.

Dip your fingers in the powder and gently run along the length of the paper from top to bottom.

You can even give it an added boost by burning the powder with incense and then letting the smoke waft over the paper. If you are submitting legal documents and fear any reprisal or are in search of a favorable outcome, use Court Case Powder to dress the papers.

When purchasing ready-made powders it is important to verify the authenticity of the brand you are purchasing the products from. Most powders don't actually contain the traditional ingredients required to make the powders a potent tool; even easy-to-obtain ingredients are not always included in those sashay powders.

Unless you plan to source every ingredient and make the powders yourself, make sure to purchase your ready-made ones from an authentic source.

Hoodoo Incense Powders

The use of incense in Hoodoo is old with direct links to traditional African religious practices as well as a part of Native American sacred rituals. Let's not forget the influence of Christianity too on the craft and the religious use of incense smoke to cleanse and bless a person and place.

Rootworkers who traditionally recite Psalms from the bible when doing a job will use incense as part of the ritual to anoint the work with smoke and bless the intentions they put forward to the spirit world, clearing the room of negativity and any unwelcome spirits.

During a job that is meant to affect a change in someone who is not present at the ritual, incense will be used as a form of transporter carrying the effects of the conjure through the smoke to the person the work is being done on.

There are also incense powders that are linked to specific zodiac signs and if a rootworker knows the zodiac sign of the person the trick is being performed on they will use that specific powder to make a stronger connection to the individual and ensure better success.

Incense is popular in conjure as a form of purification where mojo bags, talismans, and rootwork are 'smoked' by holding them over incense smoke to cleanse, purify and bless.

The Native Americans, from who the African

slaves learned a lot about nature, herbs, and spirits of the Earth, favored incense made from tobacco and herbs such as cedar, yarrow, sweetgrass, and sage. Ceremonial pipes which are an important aspect of Native American traditions and culture were smoked with tobacco while smudge sticks were made from white sage as the popular choice.

Types of Incense to Choose From

If you like doing your conjure work the old-fashioned way you can choose from the types of natural herbs, flowers, tree resin, and wood-based incense powders. These are types of incense used from ancient times and will burn while giving off a pleasant and fragrant smell.

Sage is by far the most popular herb used for incense, while sandalwood, obtained from the sandalwood tree, is both a highly fragrant and a popular type of wood chip incense; it is also one of the more expensive types of wood chip incense sold.

Resin incense is made from the sap of trees, some well-known types include Frankincense and myrrh, which were even gifted to the infant Jesus on his birth. Copal, pine, and benzoin are other types of resin incense you can obtain.

How to Use Incense

You can add a small mound of self-burning incense to a fireproof dish or vessel and set the top of the mound on fire, once it lights, blow it out and let the embers burn to let off the smoke. Or you can use a charcoal disk on which to burn the incense. The charcoal disk must be held with tongs over a lit flame, you can use your stove for this, once it lights, adds it to an incense burner or a stone burner, and as it smolders drop the incense powder on top.

Use an incense burner to carry around in case you want to manipulate the flow of smoke in a particular direction. For example, you can choose a good luck incense such as Dragons Blood powder and light it at your front door allowing the smoke to waft inward thus encouraging good luck to flow into your home. You can even add good luck incense to the soil of a plant growing near your front door to attract good fortune to your home.

Incense Blends Used in Hoodoo Conjure

There are incense blends for various objectives that you can use. A visit to a spiritual shop will reveal a whole range aimed at achieving a specific purpose. Here is a guide on the types of incense powder available and the types of ingredients included in each mix.

- **Unblocking and Clearing Incense**

This incense powder is used to clear out blocks that may be stopping you from moving on with your life. Obstacles from the past that you find hard to move can be broken by lighting this incense. You can use this incense if you are constantly doubting yourself or feel a need to gain self-worth. Typical ingredients used are white sage, ylang-ylang oil, myrrh, cloves, lavender buds, and coriander seeds.

- **Hot Foot Incense**

Quite similar to oils and powders, Hot Foot Incense is used to get rid of someone. The incense contains a volatile mix of black pepper, cayenne, red chili, sulfur, etc. Therefore, this incense should not be burned inside your house, nor must it be inhaled by you or anyone else, the smoke is not meant for. The best method to make Hot Foot incense powder work is to light it outside, or in the vicinity of the house of the person, you are targeting.

- **Love Attraction Incense**

Always a popular choice whether it is oil, powders, mojo bags, or incense, Hoodoo tools aimed at improving one's love life will always be popular. Popular ingredients used in this incense include white sage, sandalwood oil, rose oil, rose petals, buds of lavender, and other herbs.

- ### *Money Drawing Incense*

This incense is used for invoking good luck and improving your finances. Burn the incense and let the smoke waft over your purse and wallet, as well as documents and other tools linked to your finances. Included in the incense powder are fenugreek, vetiver, cinnamon, alfalfa, and other herbs associated with good luck.

- ### *Protect Me Incense Powder*

This incense can be burned for protection. You can smoke the areas around the front, back and surroundings of your home to guard against unwelcome forces. The incense can be held inside your vehicle for protection and in general, can be used on a regular basis as a protection cover. Ingredients used to make the incense include geranium, myrrh, blessed thistle, St John's wort, cloves, essential oils, and other materials that enhance the power of spiritual protection.

- ### *Uncrossing and Reversing Incense Powder*

Burn this incense to rid yourself of any hex or

curse you feel you may have been put under. Combining the burning of this incense with an uncrossing ritual will ensure better results. By using the uncross and reverse incense you are sending the curse back to your enemy. Included in the mix are powerful ingredients; angelica root, verbena, hyssop, peppermint, and calendula.

Magic Oils

Hoodoo oils are popular choices for dressing candles, bathwater, or roots. There are many names awarded to Hoodoo oils; dressing oils, formula oils, anointing oils and magic oils are some. The oils are a reflection of Hoodoo's beginnings and are derived from African, European, and Native American knowledge and beliefs.

The attributes of a plant included in magic oils are derived from its image; how the plant looks, its shape, and color influence what is believed to be its magical attributes. Therefore, oil is derived from.

The oils are aptly and simply named indicating exactly what the charmed oils are supposed to achieve.

For example, if you were seeking to do work on

someone expecting them to bend to your will, you would need the Bend Over Oil. Or if you wanted to resolve a dispute or a problem you would need Uncrossing Oil. Likewise, Reconciliation oil will help you to solve issues with your lover. Then you get the Money Drawing Oil, Kiss Me Now Oil, and Hot Foot oil the latter of which you know is used to drive away someone by influencing the magic to work through the person's feet because they have trampled your hot foot charm.

Other oils that are popular include John the Conqueror Oil which is meant to improve male virility, and Van Van oils which is extremely popular and used to dismiss hexes, and enemy spells, to manifest luck, and to increase the potency of other ingredients used in talismans, and mojo bags.

Steady Work Oil will bless the user with steady work while Psychic Vision bestows the user with visionary dreams and prophecies.

Terminology for Using Magic Oils

- Anointing—this is when you would add one small drop of oil to your fingertip, and then place it on the forehead of the person you are 'anointing' with the oil, you can of course anoint yourself in a similar manner. The term anointing will refer to rubbing oils on the body.

- Dressing—rubbing just a minute amount of oil on a root, candle, money, important document, etc. for fixing the objects with an intention. It is the same as anointing, but you say 'dressing' because it is an inanimate object.

- Condition oils and Formula oils too refer to these same types of oil in combination. A dressing oil and anointing oil will be called a formula or condition oil with the exception that at times a condition oil would be more explicitly used for dressing objects. While formula oils will include anointing oils and other perfumed formulas which are used on the body.

The Use of Hoodoo Conjure Oils

There is no hard and fast rule to say that dressing oils are explicitly reserved to dress objects and anointing oils are only for anointing the body, they can be interchanged and used with no problem.

If you wanted to bring good luck and wealth into your life you would have to use magic oil to dress objects. People who seek good fortune in games of chance, cards, and the lottery will use oils such as Fast Luck oil, Money Drawing oil, Money Stay With Me oil, and Three Jacks and a King oil. You can dress the money you intend to use in the game with the oil for prosperous results.

When seeking luck in love, dressing a candle with Follow Me Boy Oil, Love Me oil, Come to Me oil, and also Van Van oil will yield the desired results if the intentions are clearly communicated to the spirits through the burning of the dressed candle.

How to Use Conjure Oils

- As always to dispel an evil force or ill effect that has been inflicted on the body, you must use conjure oils from head to toe. Uncrossing oils can be rubbed starting at the head and down the body to finish with the evil influence being rubbed out through the toes.

- To anoint oneself with good luck spells or love spells the process is reversed, in this case, you are trying to attract luck to yourself, therefore you start rubbing the oil from your toes and up your body, all the way to the head. Keep your intention strong while doing so, or you can get the help of a rootworker.

- Healing oil, King Solomon Wisdom oil is used only on the head. You must rub the oil with the fingertips of your dominant hand. Use only the thumb, index, and middle finger.

Mojo Bags

These little pouches have symbolized an aspect of Hoodoo almost from the birth of the craft. The discreet little pouches in which you can carry charmed roots, herbs, crystals, etc. are extremely popular among rootworkers. The combination of materials tied together in a mojo bag becomes profoundly powerful as they supplement each other. Thus, the trick you are working on, or even the jinx you wish to bestow on an enemy is potent when fixed to a mojo bag. You can even carry one around when seeking out luck and money in games of chance, when attending an important job interview and when meeting a particular love interest, or to stop a vicious strain of gossip.

The mojo bag will contain a mix of magical items that are a careful combination to offer what the seeker desires. The pouch must be worn close to the body, touching the skin for it to have the desired effect.

Mojo bags are called many names; gris-gris or Gris bags, hand, a bag of tricks, nation sack, flannel, and luck ball. Gris-gris is more popular in Louisiana and South Carolina where Hoodoo originated among the African slaves.

Red flannel is the preferred choice for a mojo bag. The name *mojo* is a derivation of the West African word for prayer—mojuba. To put it simply a mojo bag is a magic spell you can carry around, a prayer, a trick, that has been enhanced with your intention. Carrying one around reminds you of the change you are trying to make and functions under the placebo effect which is the power of suggestion.

The bag offers both psychological and spiritual support to your belief. Seeing the bag feeling it against your skin and knowing there is magically working into the contents there is a great way to stay empowered and positive toward your goals, which in turn works to manifest your desires.

It is your positive energy and belief in the power of each material included in the bag that feeds the magic, making it work. Therefore, before you put a mojo bag together it is important to fully understand the power within each of the roots, herbs, etc. added to the pouch.

Typical Ingredients That Are Added to a Mojo Bag

Plants, roots, minerals, crystals,s and animal parts are all used to create a mojo bag. Bones and teeth from animals are often used and dressed with a conjure oil.

Sticks, roots, dried berries, herbs, and other parts of a plant too will be included. Roots such as High John the Conqueror are popular choices for gris bags.

Lucky charms too are added when creating a mojo bag; they include rabbit's foot, four-leaf clovers, and items that belong to whoever the bag is intended for; they can be personal items such as pieces of jewelry, fingernail clippings, hair, etc. Silver coins too are often added to a mojo bag to improve its potency.

The combination of ingredients included in a mojo bag will depend on the spell you are working on.

If you were to make a gris-gris to attract love, you would place an Adam and Eve root together with the personal effects of the person you are trying to attract and dress the bag with Van Van oil.

While dressing the objects it is important to

clearly visualize your intentions, and see them happening; thus, you will pass on your desire to the spirits that reside in the objects there. Seal the spell by lighting a pink candle dressed in a dab of Van Van oil as you prepare for the magic to take place.

If you have offered to make a mojo bag for a friend, keep happy and kind thoughts of the person in your mind as you put the bag together, infuse the charm with plenty of good vibes to make the spell work and the spirits look upon your friend with favor.

Consider the preparation of the bag a form of ritual; prepare a candle, pink for love, green for prosperity if you are making a mojo bag for attracting money. Purple candles if you are trying to battle a disruptive or difficult colleague spreading rumors about you at work. Choose the candle according to the work you are doing, dress it with the appropriate oil and then place your intentions at the altar.

The Number of Objects Allowed in a Mojo Bag

Hoodoo is based a lot on superstition as you would have learned by now. From anointing your body with oil, to cleansing and walking into a cemetery, superstition plays an important role.

When putting a mojo bag together it is important to keep track of the number of items. They must always add up to an uneven number. But the number of ingredients must be a minimum of three and a maximum of thirteen. You must count the personal items you added to the bag as part of the odd number you are trying to achieve.

Once all the objects are inside you may want to dress the bag with oil or sometimes whiskey as you would when burying a mojo bag on a gravesite.

Phases of the Moon for Conducting Successful Rituals

There are some conjurers who believe the phases of the moon have special effects on the creation of a mojo bag. Let's look at a few.

- **When Lunar Energy is at its Height—Full Moon**

Symbolizes the moon in full strength. And is particularly empowering for mojo bags created for fertility, love, healing, prosperity, and reaching success in your goals.

- **A Time for Dispelling Dark**

Conjure—Waning Moon

The two-week period from which the full moon starts to diminish in size is called the waning moon. Use this period to destroy curses and hexes cast on you or someone seeking your help. Create mojo bags for dispelling hexes, removing curses, overcoming obstacles, and solving problems.

- **A period of Low Energy—Dark Moon**

This is the phase when the illuminated face of the moon is turned away from the Earth and toward the sun. During this phase, the moon is hardly visible to us on Earth and its power is at its lowest. Due to low lunar energy at this time do not create mojo bags, instead spend the time which lasts for about three days in prayer, offering up your intentions to an altar on which you have lit a dressed candle.

- **The Birth of a New Cycle—New Moon**

The moon is still not visible to us on Earth, but it has started its transition from the new moon phase to the waxing phase. Which is the new phase you must prepare to start making your mojo bags. The new moon is an ideal time for creating mojo bags with the intention of manifesting new beginnings such as seeking a new love, changing jobs, or starting a new business.

- **Lunar Energy Starts to Increase— Waxing Moon**

This is the two-week period between the transition of the new moon to a full moon. This time is conducive to creating mojo bags with the intention of improving one's creativity, prosperity, health, and bonds in relationships.

The Color of a Mojo Bag Makes a Difference

In the olden days, gris bags were made with red flannel, however, just like the color-coded candles that empower us psychologically, today there are colors awarded to mojo bags depending on the conjure work you are aiming to achieve.

Mojo bags can also be empowered with minerals to increase their potency, they too change according to the color of the bag and the spell that is being cast. Here is a list of mojo bag colors, and the type of conjure work associated with each color.

- Blue

This color is associated with creating a calm effect in the body, it promotes serenity, and healing and increases the power of intuition. Gris bags made for healing, safe travels, and bringing about peace are made in this color.

- Black

This is considered a powerful color and therefore used for diffusing black magic. Mojo bags to reverse curses, made for protection, to dispel negativity, for justice, for vengeance, and for challenging the truth to come out are made in black.

- Brown

Represents the earth, the dirt which holds the power of the ancestors, and the power of death and birth. Brown is a humble color, it also symbolizes stability and reliability. You can use brown mojo bags to create spells for family prosperity and stability, the health of your pets, and peace within the home.

- Gold

This color symbolizes wealth and prosperity and is considered a potent color imbibed with lots of energy. Use gold to make mojo bags for success in your business, attracting good fortune, and reaching your goals.

- Green

Symbolizes new beginnings—spring, and prosperity. Use this color to create mojo bags for manifesting good luck, hope, healing, growth, achieving goals, prosperity, and changing the direction of your life.

- Red

Often the chosen color for creating mojo bags, red symbolizes the life force within us. The color also represents warnings, love, and passion. Therefore, you can use a red mojo bag for casting spells related to energy, passion, sexuality, and courage.

Making a Mojo Bag

Creating a mojo bag is a ritual, and depending on how careful you are with your conduct the potency of your spells will grow or diminish.

Create an altar for yourself before you lay out the material that goes into the gris bag. You can create an altar, if you don't already have one, by purifying a work table. Wipe it down with a mixture of salt and sulfur to cleanse the area of any impurities.

Place a candle and dress it with the appropriate conjure oil. Once done you can lay out the objects you have chosen to include in your gris bag. Light the candle and make your intentions clear, focus and let the spirits there see what you wish to achieve.

If you are not making the gris bag for yourself, placing a photograph of the person you are making the bag for will help you to focus your intention on them, thus letting the spirits too know about the person for who their help is required.

Concentrate on your intention as you start adding each item, remember to stick to an odd number. As you place each item in the bag you must thank the forces contained there. The spirit of the roots, the spirit in the crystal, the herb, and so on. While doing so never lose sight of your intention, concentrate on it right throughout, and let your thoughts wash over each object as you pick it up and place it in the bag.

While placing the objects in the bag you can recite your intentions out loud or read a psalm or prayer. It's up to you, it is not necessary to say it out loud if you are not comfortable, reciting the prayer or intention in your mind is good enough. Remember your main objective is to make your intention for creating the mojo bag clear to the spirits so they can begin to work the magic and initiate change on the spiritual plane.

Once done pull the strings and close the bag, thank the spirits for their assistance and burn any names you may have written down on paper with the flame of the candle.

Gris bags should be made with good intentions, remember the rule of Hoodoo where Left-Hand conjure is only practiced as a necessity and never as an indulgence. You must not go around cursing or hexing people just because they crossed your path, there must be a valid reason for putting a hex on someone, such as vengeance or getting back at someone for the pain they caused you. But never as an indulgence—keep in mind that whatever you put out to the forces of the spirit world will come back to you threefold, therefore, set the pace for only good returns. Hoodoo is about maintaining a balance between good and bad.

CHAPTER 5
HOODOO SPELLS

A spell is a process of manifesting your intentions.

For a spell to be successful it is important to focus on your intentions and make them clear, you must be specific about what you desire.

Remember your Hoodoo spells are working through the spiritual realm, through spirits who have come to your aid, and they need proper instructions in order to manifest your exact desires.

If you are casting a love spell, they must know the details. Are you looking for a new love, do you want an old love back, or do you want to improve an existing love affair?

Making your intentions clear will ensure the end result of the spells is satisfactory and not one you wish to undo with the greatest urgency.

Most importantly you must maintain that all-important balance between good and bad when casting a spell. Every desire you manifest through magic will come with its own string of consequences—a domino effect of change. Therefore, you must be prepared to face the challenges together with the gifts you are granted. Never take the casting of spells lightly, it is simply not a case of changing one path; your actions will of course set off a series of changes that will affect your life, and that of others connected to the change you initiate through conjure.

Casting Spells in Hoodoo

Spellcasting in Hoodoo is based on repeating your intentions as you dress and anointing each of the objects you will be using. Some conjurers will resort to repeating their intentions over and over while others will focus their minds on projecting their intentions to the objects that are being used while reciting psalms from the Bible.

Either method is acceptable provided you focus on projecting your intentions clearly. This can be done through careful repetitions of what you wish to achieve.

Choose a quiet time of the day to start your spell casting, and make sure the room you choose is free from outside noise and disturbances. Start your prayers, and psalms and focus on your intentions from the moment you start gathering the tools you will be using in the spell. Remember it can be said as a chant or verse, although chanting is not a popular method for casting spells in Hoodoo, you say it out loud or you repeat it in your mind, either way if your intentions are clear the spirits will hear them.

Reading of the Scripture When Casting Spells

Reading verses from the Bible or reciting psalms is most often practiced by rootworkers during the casting of spells. Here are some popular options.

Psalm 91 for Jinxes

This verse is read three times over when anointing a candle during a ritual to undo a curse of jinx.

Psalm 91: *He that dwelleth in the secret place of the most High shall abide under the shadow of the Almighty.*

2 I will say of the Lord, He is my refuge and my fortress: my God; in him will I trust.

3 Surely he shall deliver thee from the snare of the fowler, and from the noisome pestilence.

4 He shall cover thee with his feathers, and under his wings shalt thou trust: his truth shall be thy shield and buckler.

5 Thou shalt not be afraid for the terror by night; nor for the arrow that flieth by day;

6 Nor for the pestilence that walketh in darkness; nor for the destruction that wasteth at noonday.

7 A thousand shall fall at thy side, and ten thousand at thy right hand; but it shall not come nigh thee.

8 Only with thine eyes shalt thou behold and see the reward of the wicked.

9 Because thou hast made the Lord, which is my refuge, even the most High, thy habitation;

10 There shall no evil befall thee, neither shall any plague come nigh thy dwelling.

11 For he shall give his angels charge over thee, to keep thee in all thy ways.

12 They shall bear thee up in their hands, lest thou dash thy foot against a stone.

13 Thou shalt tread upon the lion and adder: the young lion and the dragon shalt thou trample under feet.

14 Because he hath set his love upon me, therefore will I deliver him: I will set him on high, because he hath known my name.

15 He shall call upon me, and I will answer him: I will be with him in trouble; I will deliver him, and honor him.

16 With long life will I satisfy him, and show him my salvation. (psalm 91, 2015)

Psalm 51 and 108 For Cleansing

Use this prayer for cleansing and keeping evil away from yourself and your home. Repeat the psalms three times over while making the cleansing water which you can dab on your head, back of the neck and chest/heart, hands, and feet (the significance of each of these points I have explained below).

To make the cleansing water you will need the following items.

- One glass of water

- Half bottle of Florida Water

- One candle

- Holy water which you can obtain from the church. You will find a holy water font at the entrance of the church. Or check the baptistry which will be located at the back of the church. Or you can check your spiritual supplies store.

- Purification incense powder such as Dragons Blood or Frankincense oil.

First, light the candle and make your intentions clear. You will need half of the Florida Water in the bottle, to that add the incense or the Frankincense oil, and then top it up with the Holy water. Shake the bottle to combine all the ingredients.

Once done reciting the psalms, one at a time, three times over, after which you can anoint yourself with the water.

Psalm 51: Have mercy upon me, O God, according to thy lovingkindness: according unto the multitude of thy tender mercies blot out my transgressions.

2 Wash me thoroughly from mine iniquity, and cleanse me from my sin.

3 For I acknowledge my transgressions: and my sin is ever before me.

4 Against thee, thee only, have I sinned, and done this evil in thy sight: that thou mightest be justified when thou speakest, and be clear when thou judgest.

5 Behold, I was shapen in iniquity; and in sin did my mother conceive me.

6 Behold, thou desirest truth in the inward parts: and in the hidden part thou shalt make me to know wisdom.

7 Purge me with hyssop, and I shall be clean: wash me, and I shall be whiter than snow.

8 Make me to hear joy and gladness; that the bones which thou hast broken may rejoice.

9 Hide thy face from my sins, and blot out all mine iniquities.

10 Create in me a clean heart, O God; and renew a right spirit within me.

11 Cast me not away from thy presence; and take not thy holy spirit from me.

12 Restore unto me the joy of thy salvation; and uphold me with thy free spirit.

13 Then will I teach transgressors thy ways; and sinners shall be converted unto thee.

14 *Deliver me from bloodguiltiness, O God, thou God of my salvation: and my tongue shall sing aloud of thy righteousness.*

15 *O Lord, open thou my lips; and my mouth shall show forth thy praise.*

16 *For thou desirest not sacrifice; else would I give it: thou delightest not in burnt offering.*

17 *The sacrifices of God are a broken spirit: a broken and a contrite heart, O God, thou wilt not despise.*

18 *Do good in thy good pleasure unto Zion: build thou the walls of Jerusalem.*

19 *Then shalt thou be pleased with the sacrifices of righteousness, with burnt offering and whole burnt offering: then shall they offer bullocks upon thine altar* (psalm 51, n.d.).

Psalm 108: *O God, my heart is fixed; I will sing and give praise, even with my glory.*

2 *Awake, psaltery and harp: I myself will awake early.*

3 *I will praise thee, O Lord, among the people: and I will sing praises unto thee among the nations.*

4 *For thy mercy is great above the heavens:*

and thy truth reacheth unto the clouds.

5 Be thou exalted, O God, above the heavens: and thy glory above all the earth;

6 That thy beloved may be delivered: save with thy right hand, and answer me.

7 God hath spoken in his holiness; I will rejoice, I will divide Shechem, and mete out the valley of Succoth.

8 Gilead is mine; Manasseh is mine; Ephraim also is the strength of mine head; Judah is my lawgiver;

9 Moab is my washpot; over Edom will I cast out my shoe; over Philistia will I triumph.

10 Who will bring me into the strong city? who will lead me into Edom?

11 Wilt not thou, O God, who hast cast us off? and wilt not thou, O God, go forth with our hosts?

12 Give us help from trouble: for vain is the help of man.

13 Through God we shall do valiantly: for he it is that shall tread down our enemies (psalm108, n.d.).

Psalm 118 for Creating a Prosperity Bundle

The psalm is recited over the offerings gathered to make a mojo bag of sorts for prosperity. This tiny pouch/packet containing the charms can be kept in your wallet next to your money to ensure a continuous flow of cash.

You will need the following:

- Water in a glass

- A money note(one dollar will do)

- 1. Candle

- 1. small sprig of thyme

- A small piece of orange peel

- Gold or green thread (the colors of prosperity)

Gather all your ingredients at an altar, light the candle which you can dress with Good Luck conjure oil and make your intentions very clear, while you thank the spirits that dwell within each of the pieces you are using for the spell. Reciting Psalm 118 three times over, it is one of the popular prayers in Hoodoo for invoking prosperity and financial stability.

When you have finished the prayers, place the one-dollar bill face down, then place the orange peel and thyme over the bill and fold it up into a square. Use the thread to wrap up the bundle, you must twist the thread around the packet in inward motions—wrap the thread bringing it around toward yourself, because you are asking luck to enter your life, remember you would wrap the thread outwards if you were working on a spell to drive someone away. Once sealed you can carry the pack in your wallet next to your money. If you like you can hold incense smoke over the packet before putting it in your purse or wallet.

Psalm 118: *O give thanks unto the Lord; for he is good: because his mercy endureth for ever.*

14 The Lord is my strength and song, and is become my salvation.

15 The voice of rejoicing and salvation is in the tabernacles of the righteous: the right hand of the Lord doeth valiantly.

16 The right hand of the Lord is exalted: the right hand of the Lord doeth valiantly.

17 I shall not die, but live, and declare the works of the Lord.

18 The Lord hath chastened me sore: but he

hath not given me over unto death.

19 Open to me the gates of righteousness: I will go into them, and I will praise the Lord:

20 This gate of the Lord, into which the righteous shall enter.

21 I will praise thee: for thou hast heard me, and art become my salvation.

22 The stone which the builders refused is become the head stone of the corner.

23 This is the Lord's doing; it is marvellous in our eyes.

24 This is the day which the Lord hath made; we will rejoice and be glad in it.

25 Save now, I beseech thee, O Lord: O Lord, I beseech thee, send now prosperity.

26 Blessed be he that cometh in the name of the Lord: we have blessed you out of the house of the Lord.

27 God is the Lord, which hath shewed us light: bind the sacrifice with cords, even unto the horns of the altar.

28 Thou art my God, and I will praise thee: thou art my God, I will exalt thee.

29 O give thanks unto the Lord; for he is good: for his mercy endureth for ever (psalm118, n.d.).

The Purpose of Anointing Certain Points of the Body

During cleansing or protection rituals or any other, that calls for anointing, there are specific parts of the body that need to be anointed. You must know the purpose behind this ritual in order to reap the full benefits of a conjure oil, blessed water, or powder you may be using.

- **Anointing the Head**

A person's spirit dwells within their head, therefore, it must be cleaned regularly to ensure blessings, as well as to make sure any unwanted spiritual residue has not made its home there.

- **Anointing the Back of the Neck**

In Hoodoo this area is considered the most vulnerable in terms of the back of the neck being the most accessible place for spirits to enter your body. Safeguarding this entrance with protection oils and cleansing waters will ensure unwelcome forces do not gain access to your body.

- **Anointing the Heart**

The heart is your core, your center, and bears your anxieties, fears, and stress felt by your spirit. Therefore cleansing or protecting your heart through anointing rituals will ensure it remains pure and strong enough to face the burdens of life and ground you to remain on the right path of conjure.

- **Anointing the Hands**

Your hands are your tools, they can be weapons, used to destroy or they can bring comfort. Spirits use your hands to carry out the work they are entrusted to do. Your hands will help you carry out your physical activities and will help you to engage in your spiritual work.

- **Anointing the Feet**

Feet take you on your journey of life. They must be safeguarded to ensure you stay on the right path both physical and spiritual.

Working Hoodoo spells is not complicated. Apart from making your intentions clear and reciting the psalms or prayers, there are no long and complicated verses to recite.

Making sure you offer up thanks to your ancestors and the spirits of the roots is important. Maintaining a strong connection with your heritage, your ancestors, and the spiritual world will ensure you receive help for successfully working spells.

Casting Love Spells

Love spells are among the most popular in all magical crafts and folk religions. Love is a universal need. Therefore, when someone has the power to cast a spell and bend love to their command the temptation to manipulate another's affection is high.

When casting a love spell it is important to remember that taking matters into your own hands with regards to making a particular person bend to your will and love you, through conjure, will have repercussions that are not always pleasant. When you don't let the universe decide for you and you try to force the affections of a particular person who shows no interest in you, you are making yourself vulnerable to outside forces.

Often the person you choose to cast a spell on may not be the love of your life, they may not be the person you want to spend the rest of your life with. Therefore, it is best to let the universe decide and cast a love spell that brings love your way and not the affections of a particular person who would not be noticing you in a romantic context if not for the conjure work you did.

Conditions for Casting Hoodoo Love and Good Luck Spells

- You must choose the proper day for casting spells of luck to ensure the conjure has every chance at success in love and luck.

- When casting good luck and love spells it is always best to seek out a full moon or waxing moon day which falls on a Thursday or a Sunday.

- Choose your candles accordingly. Green for prosperity, gold for riches, pink for love, and red for intense passion. Dress the candle in conjure oil choosing what's appropriate from those I have mentioned in chapter three.

Listed below are a few simple love spells you can start off with. Cast a spell for love to come your way, consider being open in your request, and work on a conjure for love and affection but leave it up to fate to decide on who that person should be.

A Quick and Popular Spell for Creating a Love Charm

You will need.

- A silver ring

- White cloth

Place the items on your altar and make your intentions very clear as you give thanks to the spirits and your ancestors. Ask for love to cross your path, but try and avoid asking for the love of a specific person who shows no interest in you. Let the universe and the spirits choose for you a better match.

Once you have made your intentions clear, wrap the ring in the white cloth. You can then dig a hole in the ground and bury the ring under the light of a full moon or a waxing moon. Offer the spirits a gift by pouring some wine over the cloth containing the ring and then cover up the hole and let the charm remain there for seven days, after which you can dig it up. Give thanks once more to the spirits and wear the ring to attract the love of your life.

Honey Jar Spell for Love

You can try casting a simple honey jar spell too as one of your first love spells. It is an ancient and very simple ritual that must be performed for seven days. Although the details of this spell are available online I will list it here for your ease.

- Dress a pink candle in Adam and Eve oil or an equivalent while concentrating on your intentions. Be very clear about what you want out of the spell, an old love back, the love of someone you adore, etc., and light the candle.

- On a piece of paper write the name of the person you desire three times, if you are casting a love spell to find love and not bend the will of someone specific you may write 'find my future husband', 'my perfect mate', etc.

- Flip over the paper and write your name three times on the back. Here again, make your intentions clear so the spirits hear you.

- Fill a jar with honey and place the paper inside making sure the tips of your finger touch the honey. Lick the honey from your fingers thinking of your intentions, being together with the one you desire.

- Seal the jar and hide it away from sight.

- Let the candle burn down and light one every week on the same day at the same time. You can burn the candle down or use a large seven-day candle for the spell.

Healing Spells

This is a quick healing spell for an injury or pain you can use to practice your power of concentration.

You will need a piece of fluorite, or if you can find one a very clear amethyst. Psalm 34 to read out.

If the pain is closer to your right hand, hold the stone in it, if it's left, then hold the stone in that hand. You can sit or lay down. Now focus very intently on what you want, healing from the pain you suffer. Imagine you can see a bright white light spooling out at the bottom of your feet.

Now, as you repeat psalm 34, take the stone and start from your feet, see yourself draw up that white light along your body. Pull it up toward your head, and let the light cover your body until it reaches your head. Now raise your hand with the stone in it above your head and see the light expand over you. Then draw the light down to the spot where you have the pain. Focus your energy on healing the pain there and continue to repeat psalm 34. Repeat the psalm three times and visualize yourself getting healed. Repeat the ritual as many times as needed and you will heal. How fast you do depends on your faith and concentration powers.

Psalm 34: *I will extol the Lord at all times;*

11 Come, my children, listen to me; I will teach you the fear of the Lord.

12 Whoever of you loves life and desires to see many good days,

13 keep your tongue from evil and your lips from telling lies.

14 Turn from evil and do good;

seek peace and pursue it.

15 The eyes of the Lord are on the righteous, and his ears are attentive to their cry;

16 But the face of the Lord is against those who do evil, to blot out their name from the earth.

17 The righteous cry out, and the Lord hears them; he delivers them from all their troubles.

18 The Lord is close to the brokenhearted and saves those who are crushed in spirit.

19 The righteous person may have many troubles, but the Lord delivers him from them all;

20 He protects all his bones, not one of them will be broken.

21 Evil will slay the wicked; the foes of the righteous will be condemned.

22 The Lord will rescue his servants; no one who takes refuge in him will be condemned.

Spell to Dispel the Evil Eye

The evil eye has a lot of influence and can affect believers and non-believers alike. It is generally born out of jealousy, or a deep-seated rage and a need to cause destruction or chaos in someone's life. A person may develop jealousy and hatred toward you merely because you have what they have been too lazy to achieve or simply lack the talent to do so. That anger, envy, and rage are all directed toward the other via the evil eye.

Protecting yourself from the evil eye and preventing its influence from entering your home can be done through the following ritual.

You will need.

- A glass of water
- One white candle
- Holy water

- Three Evil eye beads

- One Camphor cube

- Psalm 37

Place the glass on a table or altar you made, and light the candle while making your intention clear—to dispel all evil eye influence on yourself, your home, or anyone else on whose behalf you are performing the ritual.

Take the glass of water and some of the holy water to it, then the three evil eye beads, all the while keeping your intention clear. Then place the cube of camphor on top. This will float and offer its purification power to the water.

Once done you must start your prayer. Recite Psalm 37 three times over while stating your needs clearly.

Psalm 37:

26 Do not fret because of evil men or be envious of those who do wrong;

27 Turn from evil and do good; then you will dwell in the land forever.

28 For the LORD loves the just and will not forsake his faithful ones. They will be protected forever, but the offspring of the wicked will be cut off;

29 the righteous will inherit the land and dwell in it forever.

30 The mouth of the righteous man utters wisdom, and his tongue speaks what is just.

31 The law of his God is in his heart; his feet do not slip.

32 The wicked lie in wait for the righteous, seeking their very lives;

33 but the LORD will not leave them in their power or let them be condemned when brought to trial.

34 Wait for the LORD and keep his way. He will exalt you to inherit the land; when the wicked are cut off, you will see it.

35 I have seen a wicked and ruthless man flourishing like a green tree in its native soil,

36 but he soon passed away and was no more; though I looked for him, he could not be found.

37 Consider the blameless, observe the upright; there is a future for the man of peace.

38 But all sinners will be destroyed; the future of the wicked will be cut off.

39 The salvation of the righteous comes from the LORD; he is their stronghold in time of trouble.

40 The LORD helps them and delivers them; he delivers them from the wicked and saves them, because they take refuge in him.

Once done the charm or guard is now ready to protect you and your home from the evil eye. Place the glass at the entrance of your home, and make another for the rear entrance. This way your home and you will guard against the evil eye which when directed at you will get pulled into the water and drown.

You must refresh the glass of water every two weeks or as the water reduces. Top it up, take out the beads and clean them well and replace the cube of camphor.

Your talent for casting spells and conducting rituals of working conjure will only grow with your knowledge and understanding of the craft. Do not rush into any ritual or spell until you fully understand the consequences and what you will be dealing with.

Certain aspects of Hoodoo rituals can be dangerous to the foolish, it is by no means a craft to be taken merely for its ability to do 'magic'. It is a way of life and gift you will be bestowed by your ancestors as you honor and take care of their needs in the spiritual realm.

Continue to research and read as much as you can on the practice. Find an authentic root worker from whom you can learn about the ancient ways of Hoodoo. Always respect the power of spirits, maintain a relationship of giving and take and you can go on to reap the benefits of a healthy working relationship with Hoodoo.

CONCLUSION
THE MYTHS AND FACTS OF HOODOO

As you have now been initiated into the practice of Hoodoo, you already know its true nature. A folk art born out of a need for salvation, infused with the wisdom, culture, and magic of other ancient religions and ways of life.

At the heart of Hoodoo beats the roots of the African-American people, the wisdom of the land obtained from the Native Americans, and the beliefs and spirituality of the Christians.

It is a practice supported by your ancestors the slaves who suffered on Southern plantations, it is a craft held up by the spiritual world and it is in part a practice that borrows the faith and prayers of Christian teachings.

A practice of evil? A dark craft intent on causing harm?

Hoodoo never was and never will be that mythological practice created by the colonists, slave traders, and fame-hungry producers of Hollywood.

Voodoo never did and does not exist.

It is a corruption of the sacred religion of the Fon Nu people and those in Haiti. *Vodou* is a religion of power, respect, and devotion to the creators of the universe, the spirits of the land, and the people who enrich its ways.

You know the beginnings of these religions through which Hoodoo was born. You know the practice was not created for vengeance, nor was it used as such. Hoodoo was a protector, a tool used to fight back when necessary only, and to this day, that is the essence of the Hoodoo.

A Craft That Uses Both Hands

Hoodoo is a practice that requires the conjurer to practice magic with both hands, Right-Work and Left-Work, the two balance out each other keeping the equation between good and bad stable.

The practice of Hoodoo conjures, no matter how powerful one becomes, must always remain humble. You are only a vessel through which the spirits and your ancestors are allowed to conduct their work in the land of the living.

Your place is to seek them out and aid them to help you and those who need hope and pride to be brought back into their lives—just as Hoodoo did for your slave ancestors so many years ago.

Honor and respect are the cornerstones of Hoodoo, honoring the land that is energized by the power of your ancestors, giving thanks to the spirits, and carrying out the work of God through your own hands.

It is not your place to go about dispelling the myths surrounding Hoodoo, it is your place to safeguard the true nature of the practice which only a faithful rootworker will know.

Go to the crossroads and pray for new paths to be opened unto you. Use your connection with the spirit world to create a balance in your life and that of others who seek your help. Live within the boundaries of Hoodoo and you will forever be blessed.

GLOSSARY

- **Working tricks**—root work that has been activated/set in motion, a spell.
- **Divination**—the practice of interacting with the spirit world.
- **Reading-on**—Conducting a reading on a person who is suspected to be under the trick of another conjurer
- **Psalms**—sacred songs or verses from the Bible
- **Crossing**—spells to cast to cause torment, counteract a jinx for revenge
- **Hot footing**—to get rid of someone, to cause them to depart.
- **Banishment**—a spell to get rid of something or someone
- **Fixed**—to dress or anoint (candle) tool used for a spell or ritual
- **Smudge sticks**—a bundle of herbs, roots of which the tips are set on fire, put out, and allowed to smolder allowing the purifying smoke to cleanse a room or person.

REFERENCES

African Diaspora Cultures | Oldways. (2019). Oldways. https://oldwayspt.org/traditional-diets/african-heritage-diet/african-diaspora-cultures

Alvarado, D. (2009). The Voodoo Hoodoo Spellbook. In *Google Books*. Lulu.com. https://books.google.lk/books?id=ia1BAgAAQBAJ&pg=PA115&lpg=PA115&dq=hoodoo+talismans&source=bl&ots=ptMr55jafw&sig=ACfU3Uo_x6tnJcUrEu3Zex1_IP4m-vC4uw&hl=en&sa=X&ved=2ahUKEwizmcKU09b3AhXh7XMBHbS7BRoQ6AF6BAgfEAM#v=onepage&q=hoodoo%20talismans&f=false

Anderson, J. E. (2005). Conjure in African American Society. In *Google Books*. LSU Press. https://books.google.lk/books?hl=en&lr=&id=9sR_6jhCRNoC&oi=fnd&pg=PR9&ots=rZVTDgKW2g&sig=6r09fo42QAWvwe_-IoW28Egud2E&redir_esc=y#v=onepage&q&f=false

Asante, M., & Mazama, A. (2009). *Mawu-Lisa*. SAGE Knowledge; SAGE Publications, Inc. https://sk.sagepub.com/reference/africanreligion/n259.xml

Beck, J. J. (2006). *Root Doctors | NCpedia*. Www.ncpedia.org. https://www.ncpedia.org/root-doctors

Chireau, Y. P. (2003). Black Magic: Religion and the African American Conjuring Tradition. In *Google Books*. University of California Press. https://books.google.lk/books?hl=en&lr=&id=-BuLuB6sZ_kC&oi=fnd&pg=PA1&ots=aZLSYVlCY4&sig=yMQoruuYsTEbpyUdmMoxGJk9jbU&r

edir_esc=y#v=onepage&q&f=false

Conjure Oils, Hoodoo Oils, Ritual Oils, Dressing Oils, and Anointing Oils for Hoodoo Rootwork and Magic Spells. (n.d.). Www.luckymojo.com. Retrieved May 6, 2022, from https://www.luckymojo.com/oils.html

Cordin, E. (2022, May 6). *How To Cast A Love Spell [Updated Guide 2022].* The Island Now. https://theislandnow.com/blog-112/how-to-cast-a-love-spell/

Crystals, A. H. (2019, November). *Introduction to Hoodoo Magic with Crystals.* AtPerry's Healing Crystals. https://shop.atperrys.com/blogs/healing-crystals-blog/introduction-to-hoodoo-magic-with-crystals#toc_1

Definition of MAGICO-RELIGIOUS. (n.d.). Www.merriam-Webster.com. Retrieved May 2, 2022, from https://www.merriam-webster.com/dictionary/magico-religious

Ernst, M. (2014, January). *Witch 101: Graveyard Etiquette.* Crystal Crush Magazine. https://www.crystalcrushmagazine.com/magick/1-7-2021/ibphmpcgcpdi3odip54e1e5sifbcgw

Ethnicity Facts for Benin & Togo - AncestryDNA. (n.d.). Www.ancestry.com. https://www.ancestry.com/dna/ethnicity/benin-togo

Five Finger Grass. (n.d.). Freya's Cauldron. Retrieved May 9, 2022, from https://www.freyascauldron.com/ourshop/prod_6346329-Five-Finger-Grass.html

Fon | people. (n.d.). Encyclopedia Britannica. https://www.britannica.com/topic/Fon-people

Haitian Vodou. (2022, April 15). Wikipedia. https://en.wikipedia.org/wiki/Haitian_Vodou# The_nanchon

Hauser, W., Hansen, E., & Enck, P. (n.d.). *Deutsches Ärzteblatt: Archiv "Nocebo Phenomena in Medicine" (29.06.2012).* Www.aerzteblatt.de. https://www.aerzteblatt.de/pdf.asp?id=127210

Hawkins, D. A. (2021, January). *Why some young Black Christians are practicing hoodoo.* The Christian Century. https://www.christiancentury.org/article/featur es/why-some-young-black-christians-are-practicing-hoodoo

Hoodoo (folk magic). (n.d.). *Religion Wiki.* Retrieved May 6, 2022, from https://religion.fandom.com/wiki/Hoodoo_(fol k_magic)#Hoodoo_conceptual_system

Hoodoo in St. Louis: An African American Religious Tradition (U.S. National Park Service). (n.d.). Www.nps.gov. https://www.nps.gov/articles/000/hoodoo-in-st-louis-an-african-american-religious-tradition.htm

Hoodoo: Black Magic or Healing Art? (n.d.). https://english.cofc.edu/first-year-writing/Hoodoo%20Healing%20Art.pdf

Humpálová, D. (2012). *Západočeská univerzita v Plzni Fakulta filozofická Bakalářská práce VOODOO IN LOUISIANA.* https://core.ac.uk/download/pdf/295552849.p df

Incense. (n.d.). AromaG's Botanica. Retrieved May 11, 2022, from https://www.aromagregory.com/esoteric-goods/incense/

Lane, M. (2005). *HOODOO HERITAGE: A BRIEF HISTORY OF AMERICAN FOLK RELIGION.* https://getd.libs.uga.edu/pdfs/lane_megan_e_200805_ma.pdf

Lucky W Amulet Archive: Good Luck Charms, Magic Talismans, Protection Amulets. (n.d.). Www.luckymojo.com. Retrieved May 6, 2022, from https://www.luckymojo.com/saintexpedite.html

Magic Herbs, Roots, Mineral Curios: Lucky Mojo Curio Co. Catalogue. (n.d.). Www.luckymojo.com. Retrieved May 6, 2022, from https://www.luckymojo.com/mojocatherbs.html #special

Manbo (Vodou). (2022, April 1). Wikipedia. https://en.wikipedia.org/wiki/Manbo_(Vodou) #Vodou_priesthood

Moose, H. S. (n.d.). *Working Conjure: A Guide to Hoodoo Folk Magic (Paperback) | Politics and Prose Bookstore.* Www.politics-Prose.com. https://www.politics-prose.com/book/9781578636273

Oxford Reference. (n.d.). https://www.oxfordreference.com/view/10.1093/oi/authority.20110803095936832

PeopleLife. (2022, February 3). *Why do Native Americans burn incense?* Flashmode Magazine | Magazine de Mode et Style de Vie Numéro Un En Tunisie et Au Maghreb.

https://flashmode.tn/magazine/why-do-native-americans-burn-incense/

Pfingsten, M., Leibing, E., Harter, W., Kröner-Herwig, B., Hempel, D., Kronshage, U., & Hildebrandt, J. (2001). Fear-Avoidance Behavior and Anticipation of Pain in Patients With Chronic Low Back Pain: A Randomized Controlled Study. *Pain Medicine*, 2(4), 259–266. https://doi.org/10.1046/j.1526-4637.2001.01044.x

PlaceboEffect. (2021, May). Frontiers in Behavioral Science. https://www.frontiersin.org/articles/10.3389/fnbeh.2021.653359/full

Psalm 51. (n.d.). *Psalm 51 KJV - - Bible Gateway*. Www.biblegateway.com. https://www.biblegateway.com/passage/?search=Psalm%2051&version=KJV

Psalm108. (n.d.). *Bible Gateway passage: Psalm 108 - King James Version*. Bible Gateway. Retrieved May 11, 2022, from https://www.biblegateway.com/passage/?search=Psalm+108&version=KJV

Psalm118. (n.d.). *Bible Gateway passage: Psalm 118 - King James Version*. Bible Gateway. Retrieved May 11, 2022, from https://www.biblegateway.com/passage/?search=Psalm+118&version=KJV

Pslam91. (n.d.). *Bible Gateway Psalm 91 :: NIV*. Web.mit.edu. Retrieved May 11, 2022, from https://web.mit.edu/jywang/www/cef/Bible/NIV/NIV_Bible/PS+91.html

Pslam91. (2015). *Bible Gateway passage: Psalm 91 -

King James Version. Bible Gateway; BibleGateway. https://www.biblegateway.com/passage/?searc h=Psalm+91&version=KJV

Robinson, C. (2021). Hoodoo For Beginners: An Introduction to African American Folk Magic. In *Google Books*. Creek Ridge Publishing. https://books.google.lk/books?hl=en&lr=&id=o Wc9EAAAQBAJ&oi=fnd&pg=PA1&dq=cemetery +hoodoo&ots=xKyk9YXa4Q&sig=7uYrMAgAPU H1g4csJ54idqMSPUA&redir_esc=y#v=onepage &q=cemetery%20hoodoo&f=false

Shurpin, Y. (n.d.). *Chad.org*. https://www.chabad.org/library/article_cdo/ai d/4064052/jewish/Why-Wash-Hands-After-a-Funeral-or-Cemetery-Visit.htm

Slavery - Slavery in the Americas | Britannica. (2019). In *Encyclopædia Britannica*. https://www.britannica.com/topic/slavery-sociology/Slavery-in-the-Americas

The Benefits of Florida Water. (2020, August 30). Hoodoo Magic Spells. https://hoodoomagicspells.com/the-benefits-of-florida-water/

The Editors of Encyclopedia Britannica. (2015). Dahomey | historical kingdom, Africa. In *Encyclopædia Britannica*. https://www.britannica.com/place/Dahomey-historical-kingdom-Africa

Universe, V. (2021, August 24). *HooDoo How We Do: Angelica Root For Plagues and Protection*. Voodoo Universe. https://www.patheos.com/blogs/voodoounivers

e/2021/08/hoodoo-how-we-do-angelica-root-for-plagues-and-protection/

Vandal root - Valerian. (n.d.). AromaG's Botanica. Retrieved May 9, 2022, from https://www.aromagregory.com/product/vanda l-root-valerian/

Video: Black Magic Matters: Hoodoo as Ancestral Religion. (2021, December). Cswr.hds.harvard.edu. https://cswr.hds.harvard.edu/news/magic-matters/2021/11/10

Vodou, Not "Voodoo." (2010, February). Journal Times. https://journaltimes.com/vodou-not-voodoo/article_62bcf36a-1816-11df-89c6-001cc4c03286.html

VodouOrVoodoo. (n.d.). *Family helps adopted Haitian children keep their spiritual heritage.* Www.vcstar.com. Retrieved April 30, 2022, from https://archive.vcstar.com/lifestyle/family-helps-adopted-haitian-children-keep-their-spiritual-heritage-ep-369779629-350144391.html/

Wonders of the African World - Episodes - Slave Kingdoms - Wonders. (n.d.). Www.pbs.org. Retrieved April 29, 2022, from https://www.pbs.org/wonders/Episodes/Epi3/3 _wondr3.htm

Woody, B. (2019). The American Crusades: Exploring the Impact of Marine Persecution of Vodou in U.S. Occupied Haiti. *Historical Perspectives: Santa Clara University Undergraduate Journal of History, Series II, 23.* https://scholarcommons.scu.edu/cgi/viewconte

nt.cgi?article=1165&context=historical-perspectives

World Health Organization. (2021). *Obesity and overweight*. World Health Organization. https://www.who.int/news-room/fact-sheets/detail/obesity-and-overweight

OTHER BOOKS BY
HISTORY BROUGHT ALIVE

- Ancient Egypt: Discover Fascinating History, Mythology, Gods, Goddesses, Pharaohs, Pyramids, and More from the Mysterious Ancient Egyptian Civilization.

Available now on Kindle, Paperback, Hardcover & Audio in all regions

- Greek Mythology: Explore The Timeless Tales Of Ancient Greece, The Myths, History & Legends of The Gods, Goddesses, Titans, Heroes, Monsters & More

Available now on Kindle, Paperback, Hardcover & Audio in all regions

- Mythology for Kids: Explore Timeless Tales, Characters, History, & Legendary Stories from Around the World. Norse, Celtic, Roman, Greek, Egypt & Many More

Available now on Kindle, Paperback, Hardcover & Audio in all regions

- Mythology of Mesopotamia: Fascinating Insights, Myths, Stories & History From The World's Most Ancient Civilization. Sumerian, Akkadian, Babylonian, Persian, Assyrian and More

Available now on Kindle, Paperback, Hardcover & Audio in all regions

- Norse Magic & Runes: A Guide To The Magic, Rituals, Spells & Meanings of Norse Magick, Mythology & Reading The Elder Futhark Runes

Available now on Kindle, Paperback, Hardcover & Audio in all regions

- Norse Mythology, Vikings, Magic & Runes: Stories, Legends & Timeless Tales From Norse & Viking Folklore + A Guide To The Rituals, Spells & Meanings of Norse Magick & The Elder Futhark Runes. (3 books in 1)

Available now on Kindle, Paperback, Hardcover & Audio in all regions

- Norse Mythology: Captivating Stories & Timeless Tales Of Norse Folklore. The Myths, Sagas & Legends of The Gods, Immortals, Magical Creatures, Vikings & More

Available now on Kindle, Paperback, Hardcover & Audio in all regions

- Norse Mythology for Kids: Legendary Stories, Quests & Timeless Tales from Norse Folklore. The Myths, Sagas & Epics of the Gods, Immortals, Magic Creatures, Vikings & More

Available now on Kindle, Paperback,

Hardcover & Audio in all regions

- Roman Empire: Rise & The Fall. Explore The History, Mythology, Legends, Epic Battles & Lives Of The Emperors, Legions, Heroes, Gladiators & More

Available now on Kindle, Paperback, Hardcover & Audio in all regions

- The Vikings: Who Were The Vikings? Enter The Viking Age & Discover The Facts, Sagas, Norse Mythology, Legends, Battles & More

Available now on Kindle, Paperback, Hardcover & Audio in all regions

HOODOO FOR BEGINNERS

We sincerely hope you enjoyed our new book *"Hoodoo for Beginners"*. We would greatly appreciate your feedback with an honest review at the place of purchase.

First and foremost, we are always looking to grow and improve as a team. It is reassuring to hear what works, as well as receive constructive feedback on what should improve. Second, starting out as an unknown author is exceedingly difficult, and Amazon reviews go a long way toward making the journey out of anonymity possible. Please take a few minutes to write an honest review.

Best regards,

History Brought Alive

http://historybroughtalive.com/

CPSIA information can be obtained
at www.ICGtesting.com
Printed in the USA
BVHW071045130223
658402BV00018B/642

9 781914 312427